The Final Move

Escaping the Stalemate of Racism

Ray Jarrett, Jr.

ISBN-13: 978-1511752541

ISBN-10: 1511752548

THE FINAL MOVE

ISBN-13: 978-1511752541

ISBN-10: 1511752548

All trademarks are trademarks of their respective owners. Rather than put a trademark symbol after every occurrence of a trademarked name, we use names in an editorial fashion only, and to the benefit of tile trademark owner with no intention of infringement of the trademark.

Amazon.com books are available at special quantity discounts to use as premiums and sales promotions, or for use in corporate training programs. To contact a representative please order online. CreateSpace books are available at special quantity discounts to use as premiums and sales promotions, or for use in corporate training programs. To contact a representative please e-mall rjarrett@newleanstrategy.com.

This publication is designed to provide accurate and authoritative information in regard to the subject matter covered. It is sold with the understanding that neither the author nor the publisher is engaged in rendering legal, accounting, or other professional service. If legal advice or other expert assistance is required, the services of a competent professional person should be sought.

- From a Declaration of Principles jointly adopted by a Committee of the American Bar Association and a Committee of Publisher

TERMS OF USE

Table of Contents

Acknowledgments and Dedications

It is my honor to acknowledge Bishop Steve Houpe who urged me to write about my experiences. He has already blazed a trail and architected the blueprint of how to help people escape entrapments through his transparency, honesty and patient demonstration of love.

I would like to honor and acknowledge my wife, Lorna Jarrett who patiently waited for me to grow up, encouraged me to be a man of God and to be the best at whatever craft I was honing. She is my life-coach and inspiration.

I dedicate this book to my father Ray Jarrett, Sr. who was the greatest example of a man that I've ever known. I also dedicate this book to my son, Ray Jarrett, III who was named after my father and who has his own story to tell about overcoming adversity.

Introduction

> When we are no longer able to change a situation, we are challenged to change ourselves. *(Frankl, 1946)*
>
> Finally, my brethren, be strong in the Lord, and in the power of his might. *(Ephesians 6:10 King James Version)*

Initially, I didn't want to write this book.

I didn't want to write it because I was too embarrassed, humiliated and ashamed to write about what happened to me. I was too mortified to recall the events that shaped my life, my makeup and my struggles.

I like thinking of myself as a man's man. I'm sure that most men do. But when a man feels powerless to change his surroundings or the outcome of his circumstances, a little chunk of his manhood is chipped away each time something "bad" occurs.

When that happens, he may react by recoiling – he may start to become impotent when it comes to the pursuit of his goals and dreams. His life and his leadership may begin to falter.

He may attack – he may start to try and prove his manhood through destructive outlets such as anger, hostility, violence, misogynistic behavior or an attempt to control others.

He may flee – he may abandon his responsibilities by running from them and running from reality. He may leave his family, his job and abandon his friends. He may plunge himself into video games, fantasy worlds or pornography.

Or he may do all three. That's what I did.

As you read this you may fail to understand what types of circumstances could lead a man to such reprehensible behavior. On the other hand, you may have a number of reasons at your fingertips that explain the choices men and women make. Try to imagine being trapped in a dark, harrowing situation in which there is no escape. Picture yourself in the worst horror movie you've ever seen and place yourself in the role of the protagonist.

What inescapable situation am I talking about?

The feeling of being trapped. Trapped in black skin.

I am now a 55-year old man and I'm quite comfortable with the skin I'm in. I'm more that OK with being a member of the black race. I like who I am and what I have become. The dread, fear and feeling of being trapped is now gone. As a matter of fact, very few people's negative _or_ positive opinions of me actually matter. Only a select few who have my growth and best interest at heart can get under my skin – even then it's only with my permission.

But as a young, impressionable teenager in a sea of white faces, I was terrified. I would have given anything to find a way to blend in or disappear. My brown skin and kinky hair only made me a target – I felt like a hunted deer in the middle of a wide open pasture.

The Final Move

Some of the other problems, hang-ups, and issues I faced in my life were a result of life just happening. In most cases, I was the cause of my own problems. Either way, I have always prided myself in knowing the difference between racism and me-ism.

But there were times when I was minding my own business and I would hear the word "nigger" from behind me and I knew I was getting ready to take a five-against-one butt whipping from a bunch of Christians...

...the year was 1972. Did I mention that I was attending a Christian school?

When you know that you are being treated unfairly or being beaten up simply because you are black, you feel powerless. Powerless to change the situation because deep down inside you know a truth. The truth that there is nothing you can do to change the color of your skin and what you look like.

Nothing at all. As my grandfather once told me, "You were born black, you will live black and you will die black." You may cheat death and you can even cheat on your taxes if you choose to. But you can't cheat on what you look like because they can see your black face coming a mile away.

When I first started writing this book, I felt like things regarding race were getting better. With the national spotlight on the killing of African American men, one would have to conclude that we still have a long way to go. Things aren't perfect and things certainly aren't equal. I am forced; however, to admit that things are not as bad as they were 50 years ago.

The look of terror I sometimes get from the diminutive blonde lady walking to her car at night in the grocery store parking lot has in most cases been replaced by an apathetic stare or an air of false superiority. She may or may not be afraid of me because I am a large, black man. Honestly, I don't care anymore. It's not my problem. But I will admit that sometimes I smile and try to put people at ease by wishing them a good day in my best announcer / radio voice. I do that out of my loyalty and allegiance to my Christian faith and not because of any weakness or hole in my soul like the one I had when I was 13 years old.

I've talked to a number of people about the subject of racism. There are a lot more people who just don't want to expend the energy it takes to be prejudiced. They don't care. In most cases, they are keenly aware that they've been sold a bill of goods by their parents or grandparents who harbored hatred and tried to convince them that black people were unintelligent, inferior and worthy of scorn.

But that is now...

Back then, it was different. By the time I started to realize that I was the only one living by the "turn the other cheek" principle, I was 15 years old and I had suffered the humiliation of having nearly every one at the school I attended want to beat me up or "touch my hair." Some of my teachers automatically thought I was intellectually inferior – and lowered their academic expectations which in turn undermined my ability to perform, that is, until my father came to visit the school. I distinctly remember their attitudes changing when I was in 8th grade after they administered some standardized testing.

The Final Move

I remember an incident that happened after track practice one day. I was transported to the hospital after a student jumped off of a locker room bench and onto my stomach. I told my father that I got the wind knocked out of me. There were many more acts of abuse - both physical and mental - too many to recall or retell. Every day my prayer was…"Lord, just let them leave me alone today."

I told no one. Not the teachers. Certainly not my parents and not my closest friends. I told no one…

…until now. I was too ashamed. Ashamed that as a male I let this happen to me. I should have been able to stop it or to fight back somehow. I felt like a punk. There were just too many of them…

Is this a story about bullying? Somewhat.

Is it a story about overcoming racism? I did – eventually after years of covering it up with every type of emotional coping mechanism and masquerade imaginable.

Is this a story about vindication? It started out to be a journey of vindication through personal achievements, but eventually I let that go in favor or the loftier pursuit of finding out who I really was.

Is it one that indicts my parents? No. Does it vilify my abusers, and the teachers who turned a deaf ear and a blind eye to my plight? No, it is not.

It's a story of what parents should look for if they elect to send their child to a place, any place, where they are different from everyone else. It's a story about survival and finding strength during the darkest era of my 55 years on the planet. It's about the triumphs of trusting God and the perils of trusting in myself. It's a story about finding balance after living a life of excess. It's a story about hypocrisy and integrity.

It's a story about miracles.

It's my story.

Life at 1351 Georgia

Everything can be taken from a man but one thing: the last of the human freedoms—to choose one's attitude in any given set of circumstances, to choose one's own way. *(Frankl, 1946)*

My flesh and my heart faileth: but God is the strength of my heart, and my portion forever. *(Psalms 73:26)*

Life growing up as a child in the Jarrett household was idyllic. My siblings and I often referred to it as the African American version of "Leave It to Beaver." As long as you obeyed the rules, you could expect a good life.

 I was the oldest of the four children born to my mother and father and the first grandchild born on my father's side. Both of my parents came from large families; my father was part of a family of 7 children and my mother from a family of 6; each family with a rich heritage of faith. The four main tenets of our family were God, family, education and being a proud member of the black race. On any given day, we would hear something about one or more of these topics. As I stated earlier, life was good unless you violated one of the rules associated with the tenants.

For example, as a member of the Jarrett household, you WERE going to go to church. We started out in a small church on the corner of Tremont and Haskell in Kansas City, Kansas – a Church of God in Christ ministry pastored by Elder John Hannah. Later we would attend Pentecostal Church of God in Christ which has always been under the leadership of Bishop Daniel Jordan. Later, we went to a church that was associated with my high school.

I remember spending a lot of time in church. As a matter of fact, there was a period of time where we routinely spent 12 hours in church on Sundays. We also went to midweek services. My father felt like we were out of balance at that church and soon he moved our membership to another church.

Every night we would have family devotions. We would all get ready for bed, put on our pajamas and hurry into the kitchen for our "snack." We would start our devotional time by singing a song titled, "Don't forget the family prayer[1]" and then my dad would read something to us from the Bible or from our Bible story book. He would pray with all of us and send us to bed. I didn't like the singing, but the stories were always fascinating.

Education was one of the family's highest priorities. Bad grades were

---

[1] Emma L. Jackson was a staunch supporter of the music of the National Baptist Convention, Her most popular song was "Don't forget the family prayer," composed in 1945 and published in her newly formed publishing house, Jackson Studio of Music. (Boyer, 1995)

not allowed. Each child's potential was assessed and we were all expected to rise to the level of our abilities. When we got our report cards, we went "on tour." We would visit both sets of my grandparents and most of our aunts and uncles. When we got there, we were usually rewarded for bringing home A's and B's. We usually received a dime or a quarter, but sometimes we would get a whole dollar. We were encouraged to read books. My father had an extensive library; he literally had thousands of books on shelves and in boxes. This made a huge impact on me and my own family; our house is one big library – there are books in every room of the house. I later learned that there was a method to his insistence – literacy promotes classroom success. Our father's other important contribution to our educational success was that he checked everyone's homework each and every night – without exception.

We always attended family functions, dinners, reunions, weddings and funerals. My mom and dad instituted a strict family code – you never told outsiders what was going on inside the family. If someone were to wet the bed, we were all sworn to secrecy. I also had the responsibility of looking after my younger siblings and defending them at school. I was to do all of the fighting and peacemaking. Fortunately, I only had to take up for my younger sister once during my non-violent years. I was close with all of my cousins and I knew everyone's name on both sides of the family. Family was important.

I remember really understanding what it meant to be black when I was in 5th and 6th grade. Both Dr. King and Malcom X had stepped into a very prominent spotlight but what I remember most was the rise of the Black Panthers. I remember my father making us repeat the phrase, "Say it loud, I'm black and I'm proud"[2] over and over. I also remember not feeling that way at all, especially when I got to 7th grade. I remember that I was confused and angry when I was hit with the news that both Dr. King AND Malcom X were murdered. Mostly I was scared because my father sometimes practiced reciting Dr. King's speeches in the living room. I wondered if something bad would happen to him, too.

At the time, I remember not feeling exceptionally moved one way or the other about being black. We lived in a black community, I went to school with black children and for the most part, the people I saw in public places like grocery stores and gas stations were all black. Being black was unremarkable – it was just the way things were. I remember once in the fourth grade, a little white girl transferred to our school. We all stared at her because none of us had ever seen a white person in real life. She talked back to the teacher and she got lots of spankings – almost every day. This was back in the day when corporal punishment was commonplace in public school. We saw her for about 3 weeks and then she was gone. I also remember hearing that she got kicked out – her parents didn't pull her out – she was kicked out. Something about her being a negative influence. I remember seeing her legs turn red whenever she got a whipping with the ruler. I wonder what happened to her. I wonder if she ever wished that she were black.

---

[2] This phrase is the name of a funk song performed and penned by James Brown and Alfred "Pee Wee" Ellis in 1968. The song became an unofficial anthem of the Black Power movement.

The Final Move

Around the time when I was about 9 years old, I distinctly remember overhearing my dad talking about a person in our neighborhood and community who was having some financial problems. I also remember that he said that no self-respecting black person would EVER take a hand out from the government and that it was our job as a community to see to it that this family got back on their feet. We took up a collection for that family.

I never knew any black adult who didn't have a job growing up. NEVER. I just thought that was the way things were – if you are an adult, you had a job. I remember that there was one kid at school – Kevin S. who didn't have a father in his home. We all thought this was weird. I remember all of the kids at school asking him if his dad was dead. Kevin S. was considered "bad" because he was always in trouble.

I remember going with my father and his 5 brothers to play basketball at the YMCA. By this time, my uncle was a prominent, outspoken and well-known businessman in the city. Money had ceased to be a concern for him and his family. When we all came to the counter to pay to get in, the older white man said, "I can't let all of you boys in..."

That was a mistake on his part. A terrible, terrible mistake.

For the next hour or so, my father and uncles went back and forth with this man about letting us use the workout facilities. He continued to use the word "boy" when referring to my uncles and I remember thinking at one point that the police were going to have to come and rescue him. My uncles were all God-fearing men, but none of them were going to let this guy talk down or belittle them. His tactical mistake was finally relenting by saying we could come in if we all paid some amount of money. I'm sure he believed that a monetary barrier would chase us off. As a show of strength, my uncle paid for everyone to come in. I remember feeling very proud. I remember staring at the man and laughing at him – on the inside (I still had to show respect to my elders). He'd lost to my dad and my uncles. We were ALL going to go play basketball.

It wasn't so funny years later. I wasn't laughing at anyone white then.

After 6th grade was over, it would take almost 7 more years before I really knew what I had on the inside of me. It took years for me to finally be "ok" with being black.

But for the time being, life was good at 1351 Georgia. I had no worries. I ran outside and played sandlot football and kickball. In the summertime, I waited for every Tuesday to roll around; it was the day that my "Weekly Reader" newspaper came in the mail. I ate three square meals a day. I was one of the smartest kids in class, I had a good work ethic, and my father was regarded as the smartest person in our extended circle of family and community. We lived to work and earned the right to go outside and play. We did homework every day and my father checked it – every day. My mom cooked every meal from scratch and every meal was followed by a dessert treat. Lunch included. The house was always kept impeccably clean and the yard was always well-manicured.

The Final Move

We always ate dinner together and my parents were determined to make sure that we were always thankful for what God had blessed us with. My father taught us how to say the blessing over the evening meal. We had to ask to be excused from the dinner table and that was only after you'd eaten everything on your plate. If you wanted something you had to say "please" and "thank you." We didn't interrupt "grown folk" when they were talking to each other. We had chores. We were required to read two books a week. Music was on constantly at the house – either gospel or classical.

Once you learned the ropes, life was good. It took me until I was about 14 or 15 years old to master the rules and expectations of my parents – that was when I got my last whipping. Life was good for us. If only it could have stayed that way.

My Father

Those who have a 'why' to live, can bear with almost any 'how'.
(Frankl, 1946)

Wherefore the rather, brethren, give diligence to make your calling and election sure: for if ye do these things, ye shall never fall: *(2 Peter 1:10)*

My father was the second oldest of 7 children. He had a twin brother and he was clearly the most humble of the collection of my grandparent's children. I remember seeing a picture commemorating the time when Wonder Bread asked my grandparents to do a commercial for them. When you are a kid, it's fun to see pictures of your parents as kids.

My dad was the epitome of the strong, silent type. He had absolutely no tolerance for foolishness or disobedience. He meant what he said.

My father was the most loving and devoted husband I've ever known. He loved my mother dearly and the relationship I saw modeled before me was one-of-a-kind. I did not get to experience his tender side until I was much older, but I saw him demonstrate it with my younger sisters and my baby brother. We all saw it when he interacted with my mother. They cuddled, kissed and hugged constantly.

Once when I was around 7 or 8, I was at a box office window with my dad getting tickets to some event we were going to attend. The lady at the window said something to us about being handsome young men. Without ever looking up, my dad pointed to his wedding ring and handed her the money. She was embarrassed but I could tell that my father had no concern for her humiliation – she had drawn his ire. I just stared at her face – she could not wait for us to leave. This event took place in the late 1960's when a female's greatest fear was that she would be viewed as a loose woman. I didn't understand all of the nuances of what I'd just seen until much later in life, but it was a defining moment for me and helped to shape how I would come to view my father's character.

My dad would often surprise me by shedding his disciplinarian cloak and showering me with unexpected acts of kindness, thoughtfulness and _mercy_. Once when I was in high school, he dropped me off at basketball practice on a Saturday. I jumped out of the car only to look in the backseat and realize that I'd forgotten my gym bag with all of my clothes and the new shoes I'd just purchased. My father told me, "Too bad, you are old enough to be responsible for your own clothes." I remember walking in and feeling so humiliated with having to scrape together something to work out in from the pile of discarded clothes in the back of the men's locker room. I found an old white t-shirt and some plain white gym shorts that were too tight for me. I found an old pair of sneakers that did not fit. After enduring about 45 minutes of self-conscious embarrassment and incessant jeering from my teammates, my dad walked in with my gym bag. He'd driven all the way home and back. He stood there in the doorway with my bag. I was so elated – up to that moment in my life, I would had traded all the good things he'd ever done for that one act of kindness and thoughtfulness. It was out of character, or so I thought at the time, for him to abandon his mantra of accepting responsibility and the consequences of one's actions.

On another occasion, my dad let me take the family's red Volkswagen Rabbit to go to Wednesday night Bible Study. Of course, dad gave me the standard final instructions to, "come straight home after they let out..." By this time in my life, I had no problem with obedience or compliance and my life was easier for it. I'd earned my parents trust and I had way more privileges than my contemporaries at school. Besides, I knew that my mom was working nights and she needed to take the second, spare car to work. She usually left somewhere around 10:00 pm.

After church, my friends and I were standing around talking in the parking lot. If I'd gone straight home as instructed, I would have avoided a situation that I was not emotionally equipped to handle. I let some girl talk me into giving her a ride home. "It's not too far from here," she told me. This turned out to be a pattern of behavior for me – falling for a girl's sad story and tears. Open Door Baptist Church was located off of 9th and Washington in Kansas City, KS (Wyandotte County). She wanted me drop her off at a bowling alley in Grandview, MO. I could barely merge onto a highway. I certainly had never driven across the state line to Missouri and at that point in time in history, black people were not even allowed to say the word "Grandview" much less be caught lost driving around in "their" town at night. I got lost – so very lost. After wandering around for over two hours, driving the wrong way on the highway and almost running out of gas, I finally made it home around midnight.

I didn't get a whipping. Not even a lecture. I offered to relinquish my license and my driving privileges. My dad told me never to do that again and to go to bed. The next morning he lectured me on the way to school about what could have happened to me. Trust me when I say that getting off the hook was a lot like the woman who was caught in adultery hearing Jesus say the words, "Go and sin no more." Mercy.

Over the years my dad would continue to show his generosity by giving me money, cars and heartfelt advice, but I never forgot the fact that he showed me mercy and undeserved grace that night. That single act resonated with me so much that from that day forward, I found it easy to forgive others and to extend them another chance when they messed up.

By all rights, my father could have been arrogant. His intellectual resume is still impressive even to this day. He was a towering intellect with an amazing, analytical mind. He graduated from Rockhurst University with a degree in mathematics. He'd previously worked at the post office, which I'm told, was a great job for a black man back in those days. He worked nights and went to school part time until he'd finished matriculating in 1964. After he got his degree, he was hired by IBM to work as a computer programmer. My father believed in being frugal with his money and he believed in saving. By the time I was old enough to know the value of money and what it could do, I never saw my dad with less than about $1000 in his wallet...for the rest of his life. These were all reasons that he could have taken on an air of superiority with most people. He was smart, articulate, wealthy, and had a great marriage. But he was also very humble.

So you may be wondering what all of this has to do with racism. You have to understand how I felt about this great man to understand the crux of my willingness to silently endure year after year of constant suffering and ridicule. I was now old enough to notice that every person in my father's inner circle hung on every word he said. So when he and my mom sat me down and said, "I have a plan," I was all ears. I would do whatever I could – I was not about to let my father down.

You Must Be Born Again – Time to Go to School

Those who have a 'why' to live, can bear with almost any 'how'.
(Frankl, 1946)

Wherefore the rather, brethren, give diligence to make your calling and election sure: for if ye do these things, ye shall never fall: *(2 Peter 1:10)*

"Son," my dad began, "We are going to send you to Christian school. Things are getting too bad in the public school system. They have a drug problem in this district and although we have taught you right from wrong, we are not willing to take any chances with your life and your future. We also want you to be educated in a Christian environment."

I didn't have any idea what this decision would lead to, besides he was informing me of the family's decision, not asking for my consent or opinion.

I was already preparing to change schools. I had just graduated from Hawthorn Elementary and I was going to junior high school.

My parents let me know that this would be a big sacrifice for the family. My mother was going to have to continue to work nights as a nurse to make all of this happen. My job was to become a fine, upstanding Christian young man and continue to bring home the gold, that being – good grades.

Although I'd been raised in church, I really did not know anything about the process of how to get saved. I remember thinking that if you were bad, you were going to hell and if you were good, you were headed to heaven.

I attended Sunday School and learned all about the Ten Commandments and being obedient. After all, we were constantly reminded of the kids who were eaten by bears for disrespecting the prophet Elisha. Consequently, I always kept a watchful eye out for wooded areas!

Thanks to my parents, I knew lots of Bible Stories. Maybe someone mentioned the plan of salvation somewhere along the line, if so, I just didn't remember it or it didn't register.

I remember asking my mother if I needed to "get saved" since I was going to go to a Christian school. She smiled at me and said, "Yes."

At the time, we were attending Pentecostal Church of God in Christ pastored by Elder D.M. Jordan. He now holds the office of a bishop. After every sermon, he would "open the doors of the church."

"Is there one? Who will surrender their life and will to God. The bible says, behold I stand at the door and knock, if any man hear my voice, I will come in and dine with him and he will sup with me."

As a 12 year old, I had no idea what any of this really meant – even though I'd hear it many times. I know I really loved God and I have no idea why I didn't go forward before that night except that I didn't really understand what was going on and that I was too embarrassed to do it with all of my friends watching.

The next Sunday night, Elder Jordan asked if anyone wanted to be saved and I went down to the altar to do my part. The little Pentecostal church erupted. The mothers of the church surrounded me and asked me to get on my knees. They laid their hands on me and they started asking God to save me. Some of them prophesied over me. It was really loud and I was crying pretty hard. In the midst of all of that noise, I remember Elder Jordan leaning in close to me and whispering in my ear.

"Son, do you repent of your sins?"

"Yes, sir," I sniffled.

"Do you want to make Jesus the Lord of your life?"

"Yes, sir."

"Do you believe that Jesus died for your sins so that you could be saved?"

"Yes, sir."

Elder Jordan patted me on the head and announced to the

congregation that I was born again. I wiped my face and headed back to my seat. My friends just stared at me like they'd seen a ghost. I had done my part and now I could go to Christian School without being a perpetrator.

Melanin Hell High School

Many are the afflictions of the righteous: but the LORD
delivereth him out of them all. *(Psalms 34:19)*

In some ways suffering ceases to be suffering at the moment it
finds a meaning, such as the meaning of a sacrifice. *(Frankl,
1946)*

When I look back at the time I spent in Christian School, I realize that there was no way that anyone could have properly prepared me for what I was about to face. It seemed that I brought out the worst in everyone's character – both students and teachers. I often wonder if the main characters in my story even knew or realized that they were racist. I wonder what they think about when they look back and recall those years.

In some ways, I could have forgiven the younger kids because they were just being adolescents. When you are that age, you think that sticking a pencil up your nose is cool. When you have an easy target to pick on, it's hard to resist. Being black only made it easier.

The people I'd love to chat with are the adult parents and the teachers. How could they reconcile their behavior especially given the fact that they were supposed to be Christians? I now know that sin is sin and it sucks to be in bondage no matter what you are hooked on or what trips you up. To God, being racist is no different than being a fornicator.

Back in 2014, a group of ministers at our church were asked to get a shirt and collar for an elevation service. It was a special ordination service for new ministers and deacons. We were instructed to go to the Donnelly book store but instead, I went to Donnelly College. This just so happened to be the same 2-year Jesuit junior college my dad attended when he was trying to make a better life for his family. He graduated from there in 1964. He went on to Rockhurst College and graduated with honors. Take a look at the class picture I snapped while I was there. I think you will be able to easily pick out my father.

My dad went home to be with the Lord in 2007 – almost 30 years to the day of me graduating from Christian High School or Melanin Hell High as I use to call it. I actually went to two different Christian high schools; the first one while I was in 7th and 8th grade and the other from 9th until I graduated in 1977. While I experienced crippling racism at both institutions, my experience in high school was quite different from my dad's first two years of college. I never got to ask my dad why he did not consider the very real possibility that I would be mistreated at this school given its lack of ethnic diversity. I have often guessed that he must have thought I would have the same positive social and educational experience he had being surrounded by people of faith who were white.

He attended school with devout, Jesuit college students. I was going to school with pimply-faced, adolescent middle and high school Christians...not Catholics.

Too bad for me.

I was the only black face in a school of almost 300 kids. I finally spotted a dude that I though was black. He was a senior. Seniors did not speak to 7th graders no matter the color of your skin. I smiled when I saw him. He just looked me off. He had pressed his hair – I could tell that it was either permed or pressed – not naturally wavy. I was getting no help there.

Fast-forward 30 years. I remember a situation when I and another father I knew were dropping our sons off at Rockhurst College for a basketball camp. My son was probably in the 11th grade but his son was much younger. He pulled up to the curb and his son got out and ran up to the school and went in. I parked the car and went in with my son. When he saw me, he looked at me in disbelief. I got his message – why are you coddling your son? Isn't he big enough to run in? Are you raising him to be a man or what?

And because I respect him, I pretended not to notice. And because he respected me, he let it go.

But what he didn't know was that I was not about to let my son walk into that type of environment without going in and assessing the situation. I wanted the opportunity to use my well-honed survival skills to see who was against my son and who really didn't want him there. I wanted to see who might have felt the need to mistreat him. I wanted them to see that my son had a father; a real man with a chip on his shoulder. I wanted them to know they were going to have to deal with me, not his mom, if they mistreated my son.

Drop him off…it was never going to happen. No freaking way. Not to my son. Basketball is not and never will be that important.

As an adult who is healed from that, I still have some leftover residuals. I hate racism. All forms of it. Not just racism against black people, but any form of it. I prefer not to associate with racist people of any color. I might not be the person who can help you get over yourself. I know that it hurts no matter who you are and what color you are.

I also have no tolerance for bullying. I won't allow it while I am around. In the recent past, I have often dealt with the parents of bullies in a "non-Christ-like" manner. I'm sorry.

But back to the story. It's time to go to school.

The Final Move

The school must have been an old, Catholic church or something. I remember it had that old church smell to it. Kind of like old varnish. There were stained glass windows in the chapel. I remember the next year we moved into a building that had a gymnasium with brick walls not more than a foot from the baseline of the basketball court. It was probably the only gymnasium in the world that had a performance stage adjacent to one of the sidelines.

I'd never seen so many white people in my life. In person, that is. I was terrified. No one looked like me. On top of all that, I didn't know where I was going or where my locker was. For the first time in my life, I felt stupid, incompetent and overwhelmed.

We all had to go to assembly first. The hallways were crowded with kids. Some looked at me incredulously. Some of them pointed and laughed. The cacophony of voices and squeals of laughter were deafening. I quickly realized that some of the kids recognized one another from other schools. Some were in public school together. It was hard to mistake which way to go since everyone was shuttling off in the same direction. Eventually the wave of students ended in a large auditorium that was unmistakably an old sanctuary. The teachers welcomed us and gave us instructions. We sang a hymn. Everyone was smiling. Then a man (the principal I think) got up and prayed. He prayed that we would all have a good day and a good school year. I thought to myself, "This might not be so bad." I followed the other 7th graders to first hour class. On the way, I stopped at the water fountain to get a drink.

Someone shoved me. Shoved me into the raised part of the water fountain. I busted the inside of my lip. As I tasted the familiar salty taste of blood in my mouth, I turned around to see the face of the boy who would be my nemesis for the next 4 years of my life. It was R.B. I stood there in disbelief, not sure of what to do. At my last school, I would have just shoved the guy back, but I was a Christian now and I was not supposed to do those things. That would change, but not soon enough for me.

"Get out of my way, Sev-vie!"
I didn't know what the word "Sev-vie" meant.

R.B. took a drink and as he walked off he glared at me and muttered under his breath, "nigger…"

I knew what the word "nigger" meant.

The Game

I got past that first day with all of its surprises; the bus ride home, trying to make friends and getting use to the fact that I did not see the same concerned, caring look from the teachers that I was used to seeing back in grade school. Over the next few years, I experienced good days and bad days. Most days, I just felt isolated. I am convinced that during those five years of junior high and high school, only a handful of people would ever really get to know or understand me.

The "Game" was all about survival and I quickly discovered the number one non-confrontational, coping strategy when you are dealing with people, any people who think and believe that they are superior to you,…

"Discover, quickly adapt, and fit into the character they have scripted for you."

Initially, this was a very tall task for a short, skinny black kid. It would have been easier for me if my parents had dropped me off in Japan. Everything was different; the language, the lingo, and the mannerisms. To me it all sounded like Japanese.

Remember, I grew up where black culture was celebrated. "Say it loud, I'm black and I'm proud!" I didn't grow up in a rich neighborhood nor did I come from poverty. Everything was just everything. We were raised to work and work hard. Laziness was not tolerated.

So how did I recognize and deal with the fact that I'd encountered someone who thought I was lazy and had low expectations of me?

I didn't know about or even understand any of the black stereotypes that most of the white people held as gospel because in my world, (the 5 mile radius around my house) they didn't exist. If they did, my parents, teachers and clergy shielded me from them – as they should have.

I was about to get a first rate education in stereotypes. Right before I started 7th grade, a new variety show started on NBC called, "The Flip Wilson Show." This was my first insight into the differences between my culture and the culture I was forced into.

My father allowed us to watch the show, but while we did, he taught us the significance of what we were looking at. TIME Magazine featured a picture of a black man on its cover and said that Flip Wilson was T.V.'s first black superstar. My dad and our relatives were always talking about how he was using his fame for good – if for no other reason but to get the industry's best talent on his show week after week. The news often reported that it was the number one or two variety show on T.V. for the three or four years it ran.

The white people I knew only saw the entertainment value of the show. They loved it because it was funny, but also because it depicted blacks in roles that fit the scripts they'd written for us. The show fit into the mold of the collective consciousness of the white people who supported it. You don't agree? Do you think that the Cosby show would have had a successful run back in the mid-70's? They loved and constantly talked about the Geraldine Jones and Rev. Leroy characters. The good reverend was the pastor of the congregation of "The Church of What's Happening."

Well, as you might guess, the requests for me to mimic these characters came flooding in. The better I could mimic Flip Wilson, the easier my life became. Soon, I'd learned to play the role of the class clown.

About halfway through my first year, I came to discover that most people thought I came from a meager upbringing – so I let them believe it. Every day, my dad would give me $1.25 to buy a hot lunch at school. One day, I did the same thing most kids would do with the money – I spent it on candy. When lunch time came, one of the teachers saw me sitting over in the corner of the cafeteria reading a book and eating candy. She came over and started talking to me in her softest, sing-songie voice.

"Raymond, did you bring your lunch today?"
"No, ma'am."
"Do you have money for lunch?"
"No, ma'am." This was true, technically.

Tears welled up in her eyes. I fit into the role she had of me in her mind. She went over and got me a tray full of food.

For free. Sweet!

Over the next few weeks, this happened nearly every day. Some days, my parents made me lunch, but for the most part, I pocketed the money my dad gave me or spent it on candy for myself or for the people I was trying to buy friendship from. As much as I'd like for you to think I was running a slick con, I was too gullible to realize that she thought I was poor and too truthful and transparent to keep up the con when it was in jeopardy.

One day, the teacher was talking to us in Bible class. "Raymond, why don't you stand up and tell the class where your father works."

"My dad works for IBM," I proudly stated.

"And what does he do there?"

"My dad is a computer programmer AND he has an electronic calculator!"

Crickets.

The color drained from her face. I remember it like it was yesterday. But the story gets better. Or worse, depending on your perspective.

One kid in class said, "I thought you said your dad owned a restaurant?"

"He does that too," I retorted.

My father and my uncle were the only black businessmen in the city's newest mall, Indian Springs. They owned a barbeque restaurant called, "The Rib Shack." It was a hit. Every day, there was a long line of people waiting to be served that extended out of the store and down the promenade. I worked as a busboy for $1.00/hour so on the weekends. On a good weekend, I could pick up another $10 - $15. So for a while, my pockets were always full.

No more free lunches for Raymond. I was no longer the poor black kid.

More importantly, I saw how this revelation affected the way the teacher interacted with me. It also changed my status with the students.

In the meantime, my grades begin to drop.

Now please understand, most of this was my fault. I was preoccupied with my Geraldine impersonations and trying to avoid getting physically abused between classes. I'd lost focus on why I was there. I turned in my homework, but I rarely studied and managed my time after school.

The day finally came. Report card day. I opened mine and for the first time in my life, I seriously contemplated running away from home.

I got an "A" in gym.

I got a "B" in math.

I had a "C" or two and to round it off…

I had a "D" in English.

I had no idea how I was going to present this abomination to my parents. My dad's exact words were, "This must be some kind of joke."

I got a whipping and my father came up to the school to see what was going on. His first stop was to see my English teacher, Ms. H. Mrs. H. was a stereotypical English teacher in every way. She was a short, stout little old lady who wore her white hair in a bun. She wore the old-school "cat glasses" with the sparkle garnishments on the tips. She had to be all of 60 years old. She was the teacher that gave me a "D." I sat in the back of the empty classroom and my dad went to the front and stood near the desk. I was both afraid and unsure of what was going to happen next.

My dad came straight to the point. "My son Raymond, got a D in your class. I don't allow my kids to bring home D's. What does he need to work on?"

"Well, Raymond talks a lot in class," she replied.

"Crap. I'm going to get another beating," I thought to myself.

My dad didn't even look back at me. "Did he turn in his homework? I check it every night…"

"Oh, yes," she replied, "it's all here."

"What did he get on his tests?"

Without looking at her grade book she peered at my father over her glasses and said, "As I recall, it was mostly "B's" and "C's.""

My dad looked puzzled. He whipped out a pen and started asking questions. "Tell me exactly what grades he got."

She tells him.

"That doesn't add up." I could hear the cold steely tone in my father's voice.

And she said...

"Yes it does. It just came out to be a D..."

Oops!

Wrong guy lady. I remember hearing something about injustice and I was asked to step outside. When my dad got back, I was on the bubble of a B- / C+. Of course, she gave me the C+. During the ride home, I got a lecture that lasted until we pulled into the driveway.

"Son, MAKE them give you an 'A'... Never let your work be so close to the edge that they can down grade you or take anything from you. If you want to be successful, you can't just be as good as everyone else – you have to be better."

No pressure, here.

This was the other distasteful part of the game. My days of just being a normal kid were over. The more I tried to forget about that reality, the worse my experience became. There was now no such thing as equal ground. I was going to have to be better than everyone else around me to get what I deserved. How long was this going to go on? What if there were just some people that were smarter than I was? What then? Later in my life, I would discover the Great Equalizers – hard work and determination. For now, I was just determined to make sure that my dad never had another occasion to come up to the school. That event would be the closest that my dad would ever come to knowing what I was going through.

So that was the end of my employment at my dad's restaurant on the weekends. Besides, they'd caught my cousin, the other bus boy, stealing out of another employee's purse. Caught him red-handed. From that point forward, no under aged kids were allowed to work in the restaurant. You had to be 16. Too bad, I'd earned the reputation as the hardest worker there, bar none.

By day, I was a performer of sorts. Performing for my school mates and teachers. I was being beaten and ridiculed. I was called "nigger" every day. They asked me stupid questions – every day.

"Why are the palms of your hands and the soles of your feet white?"

"Why does your nose look like that?"

"Can I touch your hair?"

A girlfriend was out of the question – this was the mid 70's. That part of my social development would have to wait.

By night, I was still the golden child who seemed to have everything going for him. I still lived in a black community and I still had black friends. Again, I never told my dad anything. Never mentioned a word to my mom. The bus rides home were the worst. At least while we were at school, the teachers were there to keep the wolves at bay – at least that is what they were supposed to do.

While all of this was going on, my parents were still enriching and enhancing my black education. I was learning about Medgar Evers, Malcom X and Dr. King. My father wanted me to understand and comprehend each person's message. He stressed that they were all different and black people needed to hear what all three had to say. But I also remember thinking that anyone who did good things was going to be murdered. People like Jesus, Lincoln, Evers, Malcolm X and Dr. King all met with the same fate.

I just knew that the people at my school were going to kill my dad.

I told myself, "I can't have my dad coming up to the school again. Ever. I'll do my part. I'm ready now. I won't let these white people kill my dad."

By the time I'd reached 8th grade, I didn't feel much like being black and I certainly didn't understand Christianity. How could these people treat me this way and still say that they were saved? Saved from what? Why did I have to act right and not them?

But all of these things taught me how to play the game.

I can read a face like I'm reading a book. I know how to pretend like I don't know what is going on. I know how to give off the right signals to those who are as perceptive as I am to let them know how I feel without saying a word. I learned how to bait people into telling me how they feel about black people; I learned how to get them to let their guard down. I can spot someone who has an air of superiority a mile away. I can smell racism even in its most diluted form. The key to the game is not to let them know that you know their dirty little secret.

I can tell if you like me or if you don't. I can tell if you are pretending to like me. Most importantly, I've learned to listen to what you are saying – and not saying. If I can listen long enough, I can tell what you think of people like me and what mold you think I should fit into.

These became the tools for my survival. They kept me safe. They kept me from walking into dangerous situations. They let me know who I could trust. They would serve me well later in life. A few years back, I read a quote about "playing the game,"

"The sacred stillness of your brilliant heart has as the myriad wonders masqueraded. But if you knew this secret from the start, then you'd have quit this Game before you played it." (Leventhal, 2012)

An old Italian proverb states, "Once the game is over, the King and the pawn go back in the same box."

How I longed for a life of innocence where I never knew "The Game" existed and where I certainly was never required to play it.

The Good

There was some good that came from this acerbic, festering pool of negativity. A lot of good, in fact. Despite the duplicitous behavior of most of the Christians and some of the teachers, the spiritual foundation I got at the school was worth the trials I had to endure. For my first two years, we were required to memorize a passage of scripture every other week. Sometimes it was 3 or 4 verses and sometimes it was a whole chapter. We received a great deal of intense bible teaching and although some of it was flawed, most of it helped me to endure what I was going through. I find it both ironic and providential that the very place I was being persecuted was also the source of my strength. There were a couple of teachers who empathized with my plight and they often gave me a sense of hope that I could carry on. If fact, there were a couple of teachers (after I was older) that took a special interest in me. This oppressive environment helped me to move forward into a future life of helping hurting people.

I can't explain why I didn't immediately start lashing out. I didn't attack the ones who were attacking me. I don't know why I just didn't give up and start tanking my grades and classes. At the first sign that I couldn't handle the academia – maybe my parents would have taken me out of the school. As a matter of fact, I know if I'd told them what was going on, I'm sure they would have moved me out of that particular school.

All I know is that at that time, I believed with all of my heart that the Word of God was true and that everything contrary to the Word was wrong. I was afraid of failing, afraid of letting my father down, and afraid of going to hell so there was no way I was going to start acting like them. Unfortunately, I could not sustain my conviction as I got older and I would inevitably turn my back on these principles.

I talked to God constantly. By the time I was a senior in high school, I felt like God was granting my every request and wish. I still wonder why I abandoned this kind of life to live by my own set of rules.

Persecution can be everything or it can be nothing. Persecution for the Word's sake that inevitably develops Christian character is worth everything; at least I would have felt like I was enduing for a good reason. Persecution for something as idiotic as racism is nothing – it is meaningless. The instant I abandoned my commitment to the Word in order to do my own thing, I had no reason to endure persecution of any kind. And I didn't.

I remember attending chapel services each week and listening to all of the marvelous speakers that came to visit and speak at our school. There were missionaries that came to us with fascinating stories of the work they were doing and all of the great miracles they'd seen. There were special guest musicians who came and taught us new worship songs. There was even a team of men who performed feats of strength and gave their testimonies. I hung on their every word. I imagined that if they were teachers at my school, things would be different.

I also imagined that R.B and all of my other tormentors would hear one of these marvelous sermons, want to go to the alter and surrender their lives to Jesus. I thought that if they did, the same Jesus that kept me from retaliating would keep them from abusing me. Unfortunately, that day never came and eventually I decided to take matters into my own hands.

I still hold the scriptures in my heart. I remember the sermons with clarity. I see the faces of my true friends. I know that some good came from my experiences.

I'm often asked the age old question; if you had it to do all over again, would you?

The simple answer is "Yes" but it requires an explanation.

The problem with going back is that you don't know how the changes will affect the outcome. I have to assume that avoiding the abuse would result in me developing into a well-adjusted adult. But that still leaves me with the problem of navigating around the pitfalls my parents wanted me to avoid. Most importantly, there would have been no impetus for me accepting Christ as my personal savior. I may well have never taken that step. I just don't know.

My only clue is to look at and consider the lives of my contemporaries who did not attend private Christian school. When I approach the question from this perspective, I can offer a final conclusion. Storytellers down through the ages often warn of the unintended consequences of going back in time with the intent of making things "better." This reminds me of a story from the Star Trek "Next Generation" series. I promise to tell the "non-trekkie" version of the story to succinctly illustrate my point.

The captain of the starship Enterprise, Jean Luc Picard, was injured in an ion storm while he was on a mission. The electricity generated from the storm caused irreparable damage to his artificial heart. As the captain lay dying, we see him drifting in and out of consciousness. In this near death state, an alien being named "Q" appears to him and initiates a conversation about his life and his choices. The captain starts a back-and-forth debate with "Q"; they clearly do not like one another. The captain has had many run-ins with him and he has grown to loathe and despise "Q". "Q" is an alien with nearly limitless power, yet he often abuses it on frivolous pursuits and arguments; mostly at the captain's expense. "Q" really does have a soft spot in his heart for the captain and crew of the Enterprise, but often puts the whole of humanity on trial for not living up to his expectations.

During their conversation, "Q" tells Picard not to blame him for his condition – he reminds Picard that it was his own impetuous and cocky nature as a young cadet at the academy that ultimately caused his current predicament. Picard got involved in a bar fight that ended badly for him and in the end, he was stabbed in the heart. The young Picard had to have emergency surgery, and to save his life, the doctors gave him a mechanical, artificial heart.

The captain reflects on the event and realizes that "Q" is right.

"Q" asks, "Do I hear a regret?"

"I regret a great many things from those days," Picard replies.

Presto Bingo. Now we see the captain 25 to 30 years in the past...just a few days prior to the infamous bar brawl. His primary task is to avoid the fight that got him impaled through the heart. If he does this, he gets to return to the present and continue his life unfettered by a heart that could potentially lead to his untimely death. The episode adds a nice twist to the story in that all of Picard's friends see him as a young cadet; however, when he looks in the mirror, he sees himself as the older and wiser Picard – and he acts and conducts himself accordingly. He exercises the right actions, but in the wrong season of life.

This perspective guides his actions and he begins to unravel every relationship of value he has created. By the time the life-defining altercation rolls around, Picard has managed to destroy every friendship he's created. All of his closest comrades have abandoned him.

Poof!

Picard is back in the present only now, he is no longer a starship captain! In fact, he is not even an officer. His out-of-season predilection for taking the safe, sensible path has perpetuated itself throughout the tapestry of his life and now he is a shell of himself; a menial, servile man who toils in obscurity. Try as he might, he cannot convince the others that he is capable of more. He has become, in his own words, "a man who is bereft of imagination and passion." He appeals to "Q" to give him back his old life even though it may cause his untimely demise. (Landau, 1993)

I am who I am because of the sum total of my experiences. Would I have "tapped out" if given the choice at that time? Probably. But when I look back, I can say that the strength I have is partially because God walked with me through this tough time.

If I must endure hardship, I also want to reap the rewards of the maturity process that comes as a result of weathering the storm. There were some good things...life turned out way better than I thought it would. I'd rather work through my issues instead of avoiding them and forfeiting what I've learned about life. My experiences made me successful and they pushed me closer to God. They made me tougher and they've equipped me for what I have to do.

The Gullible

Impressionable. Unsuspecting. Unsuspicious. Unwary. Ingenuous. Innocent. Inexperienced. Unworldly. Green.

The synonyms of the word "gullible" describe the young man that I once was.

This trait turned out to be a huge blessing in the end.

If there is one thing I've learned is that gullible and girls don't mix well. In fact, being gullible can lead to a lot of issues but there is one more word that belongs in the list of "gullible" descriptors.

Innocent.

I was young, my heart was pure and I believed what people told me. It was inconceivable that someone would purposely lie to or deceive me. As the old R&B song says, "A child is born, with a heart of gold, the way of the world, makes his heart so cold." (White, 1974)

One day a girl named Nancy started being nice to me. I started being nice back. During class, we started passing notes to each other. We were just friends. That's all I knew how to do in seventh grade anyway. Nancy asked me if I was coming to the school Halloween party / Haunted House event that evening. I said yes. She smiled and said we could go through the Haunted House together. This all happened around second hour. By the end of the day, I discovered that Nancy's demeanor towards me had cooled considerably.

Now that doesn't sound like it has anything to do with race or color, does it?

Later that year, I found out that her friends and the teachers highly discouraged her from "being my friend." It actually took the Sadie-Hawkins banquet for me to find out why.

Jim was a good friend of mine. He was not "in" with the popular mainstream crowd at the school, so it did not hurt or cost him anything to be my friend. It just so happened that we took an interest in the same girl – Janice. The only cross words we would ever have would be over this particular girl. We both wanted to go with her to the dance. Badly.

As it turned out, Janice, who was an 8th grader, was holding out for a guy named Bruce. Jim and I were out. We started speaking again because Janice was now our common enemy – she'd spurned us both. After all of this blew over, Jim said a strange thing. He said, "I don't think you could have taken her out anyway because of your color."

That did not sound right to me. It didn't make any sense.

Now mind you up until that point, I never heard anything about any taboos related to mixed race dating or friendships. My parents exposed me to a great deal of the "black struggle" but never made mention of who I could or could not date. I never found out if this was by design or if they though that I was just too young to be thinking about dating. I looked Jim squarely in the eye and told him, "There is no way that can be true, you just don't want me to take her to the dance."

Fast forward a couple of months. We'd just heard a good sermon from one of the chapel speakers. So good in fact, that Jim and I decided we trusted him enough to answer our question about interracial dating. We both ran up to the minister and asked him, "Is it alright for black people to date white people?

"No," came the reply.

"Why not?" I asked, "Is that somewhere in the Bible?"

That's when things got weird. He turned to the scripture that commands us as believers not to be unequally yoked.[3] Yes, I know that seems far-fetched, far-reaching and far-out but I recall him saying it with a straight face. But Ray, "The Gullible" took it hook, line, and sinker at the time. I wonder how he felt later in his alone time with God knowing he'd misused the Word of God to deceive a young, innocent Christian. He mishandled God's word to support his racist beliefs. He would have been better off just telling me that _he_ didn't think it was right.

---

[3] Be ye not unequally yoked together with unbelievers: for what fellowship hath righteousness with unrighteousness? and what communion hath light with darkness?
2 Corinthians 6:14

The scriptures say, "These little ones believed in me. It would be best for the person who causes one of them to lose faith to be drowned in the sea with a large stone hung around his neck."[4]

Most of my hurt came from being unsuspecting and overly trusting. At the heart of the matter was a belief that all of these people were supposed to be Christians. Where I came from, I'm sure there were some sinners, but I knew they were sinners because they professed to be sinners. They didn't come to church and they would tell you that they weren't coming. These "new people" in my life were professing that they knew Christ and at the same time they were treating me differently because I was black.

I respected R.B. More than all of the others combined. Truth be told, I knew if he got a chance, he was going to kick my butt. He called me a nigger to my face. He wore every prejudice he had on his sleeve and he let me and everyone else know about them. I could tell that he wasn't so sure about all of this Christianity stuff. The others, especially the teachers who professed Christ and somehow justified their prejudices - were deplorable in my eyes. I remember them standing by and doing nothing to stop the madness. I was never a tattler, but other sympathizers, who had no interest in being my friend, were at least real about their faith. They let the teachers and administrators know what was happening. Still nothing.

---

[4] Matthew 18:6, Mark 9:42 and Luke 17:2

There was one teacher who seemed to like me. Our drama instructor was much younger and seemed to be more progressive than the other teachers, but in the end, he proved to be worse than all of the rest.

Throughout most of Mr. H's class, I got a menial parts for the plays we participated in. I always volunteered, but I could never get anything of any substance. One day Mr. H came in and gave me a part to read; it was a lead part. It was a soliloquy and he was giddy with excitement for me to read it. I was an excellent reader, but I couldn't make out most of the words. Is seemed as though it was written in another language. I sat next to the teacher while he laughed at my attempt to get the words right. I told him I'd go home and practice and I'd be ready for my reading in front of the class the next day.

I was excited! I could not wait to tell my dad and mom that I had my very own soliloquy! My dad told me to practice. I came in to read it to him when I thought I was ready.

I remember it like it was yesterday so I was able to easily find a copy of it on the web after a quick search for some key words. Before you read on, I must warn you that the following text is extremely offensive. It isn't vulgar – but it makes you wonder how anyone can write something like this and moreover, how a Christian teacher could give it to a little impressionable black boy as a source of personal entertainment. I'd never seen anything like this and I'd never heard anything like this at the time. I'd never heard anyone talk this way before so I did know it was supposed to be derogatory or offensive. I was in the seventh grade. I was innocent and very gullible.

But the teacher knew exactly what he was doing. Here is a copy of the text.

"The Sermon of the Peasle Tree"

"Brother'n and Sister'n, I's been so took up dis week wid de pastoral duties 'mongst de flock and gleanin' in de vineyard of de Lawd, dat I ain't had time to give to de preparation of no real theologic sermon. I's gwine let de Bible drap open and wheresoever my eyes rest, I'll know dat de Lawd has guided me to dat text to hold forth to y'all's dis mornin'.

"My eyes rest heah, Brethen and Sistern, at de text as recorded in Two Eye Kings, whar de text say dat "de Chillen of Israel worshipped De Lawd wid de harp and wid de instument of seven strings and wid de ... uh ... wid de ... uh ... p s a l t r e.' Now, Brethen and Sistern, de text say dat 'de Chillen of Israel worshipped De Lawd wid de harp and wid de instument of seven strings and wid de ... p s a l t r e ... and wid de Peasle Tree!

"Now, my text dis beautiful Sabbath morn will be de Peasle Tree! I's gib a great deal of thought to study of de history of de Peasle Tree. De Peasle Tree was a tree what grow up in Moses' backyard down in de land of Egypt.

"And, when de Peasle Tree is growed up and flourish like de young shade tree, Moses went out in de backyard and he took his two bit Barlow knife

... de one dat has four blades and a beer opener in de back ... and he cut hisself a staff off'n de Peasle Tree and when he has skinned de staff up good and smooth, de Lawd spake unto Moses and he say, "Moses, take thy Peasle Tree staff in thy hand and put thy food in de middle of de big road leadin' on down to of Mr. Pharaoh's house!

"Now, Brethen and Sistern, Mr. Pharaoh was quality white folks in dem parts, in dem days. But Moses, he ain't paid no mind to dat 'case he knows dat de Lawd was 'hind him and he walk big and cocky, like de Lawd want all his people do when dey know dat de Lawd is 'hind dem in what deys doin'! And, besides of dat, Moses was a meekest man dat eber lived and he played on de harp wid a thousand strings, spirits of righteous men to make perfect!

"And, Brethen and Sistern, Moses jus walk rite up to front door of Mr. Pharaoh's house and knock on de big brass knocker door. And, when Pharaoh's boy come to de door, he say, 'What you want, Moses, come round heah knocking on white folks' front door like dis?'

"Pharaoh was a proud man, he don' like to hab people knock on his front door. And, Moses jus' say, 'I wants to see Mr. Pharaoh!' And, de boy say, 'Mr. Pharaoh claim dat he ain't in dis morning.' And Moses say, 'I knows dat he's in case I sees his saddle house hitch out here at de hitchin' rack!' And, he talk to him like dat, Brethen and Sistern, and he turn't Moses in to see Pharaoh. And, Mr. Pharaoh say, 'Moses, what you doin' pesterin' me like dat, in de middle of de mornin' when you knows dat a gentleman ain't s'posed to be done drinkin' his mint julep yet?' And, Moses said, 'Pharaoh, I wants you to turn dem chillen' loose!'

""What chillen' you talking' bout?' say Mr. Pharaoh. Moses say, 'Now, Mr. Pharaoh, don't you try to act all bigens wid me! You knows I's talking 'bout dem Chillen of Israel, I want you to turn loose!'

"Pharaoh say, 'What you doin' talking 'bout dem Chillen of Israel? Didn't I gib 'em a day off on George Washington's birfday and didn't I gib 'em Fouth of July off? And, ain't de cotton and de corn jus … and de 'bacca and all dat … jus plum filthy wid weeds? Ain't gwina gib 'em no more day off!'

"And, when Moses see dat Pharaoh is hard in his heart, 'gainst him like dat, Moses jus drop de Peasle Tree staff on de ground and it turn into a fiery serpent! Pharaoh jumps back from de fiery serpent … he scared! Moses jus retch down and pick up de fiery serpent by de tail and strip it 'round his head three times for luck and make a cross on de ground and spit in de middle of it, take de conju'e off, and turn back into a Peasle Tree cane!

"Pharaoh say, 'Now look here, Moses, whilest you was talking, I been studyin' 'bout dis thing, let's talk reasonable 'bout did now! Dem Chillen of Israel is powerful poor field hands anyhow and dey done et dere heads off many times over. Dere hardly no rations left in de land for my own people … gwine turn 'em loose!'

"And Moses jus pick up de Peasle Tree staff in his hand and walk on down to his house. And he say, 'Call in all de hands, dig up de Peasle Tree, wrap de roots up in a guana bag and put in one of dese heah Studebaker wagons, hitch four of dem big Missouri mules to it, don' you hitch none of dem shackled in cotton field mules to dat wagon! We's gwine march out

of Egypt wid a high hand!'

"And, Brethen and Sistern, de Chillen of Israel all march on down de Red Sea road, right in de middle of de mornin', wid red tassels on de mules' hames, and a New 'Nited States flag flying from de topmost branch of de Peasle Tree, and de Lawd smilin' down on de whole procession!

"And, when dey gets to de Red Sea, de Chillen of Israel look and dey say, 'Moses, ain't no ferry and ain't no ford ... how we gwine get across? Now, jus look at de mess you and de Lawn done got us in, jus look at de mess you got us in!'

"And, Moses, he jus cool as de center seed of a cucumber! He wave his hand seven times from de East to de West and de wind blow de leaves of de Peasle Tree, and blow de Red Sea back and de chillen march over on dry foots!

"And when dey get over on de other side, dey look back and dey see de hosts of Egypt followin' 'em and de Chillen of Israel scared and dey huddle 'round Moses like sheeps round a shepherd dog. But Moses, he ain't a'scared and he jus turn 'round and he wave his hand back de other way seven times from de West to de East and de wind blow back thru de leaves of de Peasle Tree, and drown all de hosts of Eqypt!

"And forty days and forty nights de Chillen of Israel dey wander in de wilderness. And one mornin' Moses wake up and he go down to de stables and he see de mules hain't been curried and de Peasle Tree hain't eben been watered! And Moses cuss de stable boys for all dere sorry ways of doin'!

"And den de Chillen of Israel mummer 'gainst Moses and dey say, 'Moses, we's hongry, we ain't had no rations issue us dis month!' And, Moses jus say, 'Go on out dere to de Peasle Tree and eat peasles!' And, Brethen and Sistern, dey pick us twelve baskets of full of good ripe peasles! And 'tis recorded, both in de sacred history and all de profane history, dat dey set down to possum and sweet 'tater wid brown gravy!

"Some folks said dat it was manna dey et in de wilderness. Nothin' t'all but peasles! Some folks said a pillar of fire by night and a pillar of clouds by day guided 'em. Nothin' t'all but jus de moon shinin' on de leaves of de Peasle Tree at night and de shade of de Peasle Tree in de daytime!

"Brethen and Sistern I says unto you, verily, verily in dat last great day, when de Angel Gabriel shall come and de earth is rolled up like de ol' newspaper and cast on de fiery flames to burn, and de sheeps is gathered on de right and de goats is gathered on de left ... Brethen and Sistern, in dat day if you 'spects to take yoah place on de right and be told off by Saint Peter whilest you march thru dem Pearly Gates and walk on dem golden streets wearin' dem golden slippers, Brethen and Sistern you must be found wearin' a right smart size bunch of peasle leaves in yoah pocket! Amen!" (Willis, 1946)

I got as far as the first paragraph and my father snatched the paper from my hand. He yelled, "Who gave you this, who gave you this? You are not reading this, do you understand?!!" He left the room and went back to talk to my mother. When he came back, I knew he was going to the school. I pleaded with him not to go,…well a little bit. I did not want my father to think I was challenging him. I liked Mr. H. I didn't understand why my dad was so angry. He never told me. I found out later why he was so angry. As an adult this event caused me to do something I've never done before and that I've never done since - and that was to question my Father's decision to leave me in Hell...

Melanin Hell.

From the 9th grade on, I constantly asked my parents to let me leave Christian school.

Ball is life and intellect is everything

Don't aim at success. The more you aim at it and make it a target, the more you are going to miss it. For success, like happiness, cannot be pursued; it must ensue, and it only does so as the unintended side effect of one's personal dedication to a cause greater than oneself or as the by-product of one's surrender to a person other than oneself. Happiness must happen, and the same holds for success: you have to let it happen by not caring about it. I want you to listen to what your conscience commands you to do and go on to carry it out to the best of your knowledge. Then you will live to see that in the long-run—in the long-run, I say!—success will follow you precisely because you had forgotten to think about it. *(Frankl, 1946)*

Completely by accident, I found out how to keep the wolves at bay. I also thought that I'd found a way to get people to like me.

It was actually just a continuation of what I'd gotten away from in grade school. My class clown behavior was getting me nowhere except in trouble. If I concentrated on making good grades, at least I would gain some measure of respect even though I would never win anyone's admiration or love.

I didn't really start buckling down on my studies until I was in ninth grade. Both my seventh and eighth-grade years were filled with episodes of abuse and readjustment. After 8th grade, I transferred – or rather my parents transferred me – to another Christian school that was closer to home.

In my eighth grade year, I was introduced to one of my greatest loves. She was round and she was orange and black. Her last name was Wilson... Or was it Spalding? She was a basketball.

Basketball served a great purpose in my life. It was the great equalizer. This game, combined with academics, were the only two places where my race did not matter. I could control my destiny – up to a point. In eighth grade, all I did was ride the pine. Ninth grade was not too different, but that is when I begin to develop a love for the game. The next year, I worked at it constantly and by the time my 10th grade year rolled around, I was a decent ballplayer.

Tragedy struck my basketball career in my junior year. I was diagnosed with Osgood-Schlatter disease. This condition afflicts adolescents that experience a growth spurt while participating in sports. My case was severe. I'd grown 8 inches in one summer.

In what would be my first act of faith, I miraculously recovered and played basketball my senior year. That year, I was named the MVP of my team and I was also named the recipient of the Jerry Ingram Christian Athlete award.

If it sounds like I'm taking a very perfunctory approach to describing my early basketball career, it's for a reason. I now see perfectly the role

54 | P a g e

basketball had in my life.

You see, while I was out on the court, I had a legal way of getting back at my tormentors without using my fists. Even though I didn't have plays designed for me and my teammates didn't always pass me the ball when I was open, I was still able to score and more importantly, I was able to initiate aggressive, physical contact by rebounding on both ends of the court.

I learned early on that you don't really need anyone to pass the ball to you to get "touches." If you really want it – you can go get it whenever you want by wearing your opponent down with defense and learning the art of stealing and rebounding the basketball at both ends of the court. By the time I enlisted in the Air Force, I could take the ball from most guards five or six times a game. Rebounding meant that I got to push on you, pull on you and punish you. It was easy to get 10 to 12 boards a game in our small Christian league.

But honestly, I could've cared less about my stats and truth be told, I loved the game for what I did for my self-esteem, not just for love of the game. I was not going to let anyone beat me on the court... ...or in the classroom.

The classroom was my place to get back at the teachers. By the time I was a senior, I was obnoxious and incorrigible. If I had to study all night to get an A, that's what I did. After a while, just getting an "A" wasn't enough – I wanted a 100 on my tests; I wanted perfection. I did exactly what my dad told me to do earlier in life; I made them give me an "A."

During my senior year, I was particularly interested in tormenting my English teacher. Each day when I walked out of his class, I would ask him "Who's the greatest? Who has the best GPA in your class? Who's the best - huh?" Sometimes I'd even do an Ali impression on him by asking him, "What's my name?"

Some days he was amused and some days he was annoyed but mostly he was, "astonished out of measure" only because he incorrectly assumed that the other kids were smarter than me...

... and they may have been. But on paper, the best they could ever hope to do was to match me. This was unlikely because they had nothing to prove – no reason to stay up until midnight studying. I did. So not only did you have to be smarter than me, you would have to outwork me too. And that, my friends, was **_never_** going to happen.

Even when I got to the corporate world, I realized that as long as raises and promotions were based on merit – I'd always be amongst the top performers - if not the top performer. Why? Most people don't want to put in that kind of work.

One day, I was talking in class as usual. My father had taught me to always be a couple of steps ahead of the teacher so that when they got to the next topic, it would not be the first time I'd heard the material. In Mr. L's class (the American literature teacher), I was about three chapters ahead and I had already answered all the questions at the back of the chapters. This class was not really "work" for me since I loved reading.

This particular day, Mr. L. had enough.

"Jarrett — you think you can just show up to school and play basketball and talk in my class? You are going to flunk this next test."

The other students just laughed.

"You don't know who I am, do you? I don't flunk tests. As a matter of fact, it will be your hand that writes an "A" at the top of my paper."

"Jarrett — go to the principal's office."

This was no sweat off my brow; that particular principal happened to like me. Too bad he only lasted for a year at that school. He was not racist. We'd often sit and chat about the things I was going through. The truth is, by my senior year, I wasn't going through too much. Things had shifted from the obvious overt racism to the more subversive form that most of us are familiar with.

My high school basketball career was going well, but in the end, I fell short of my academic goals. I found out during my senior year I had a lock on becoming the valedictorian of my class of 1977... or so I thought.

Our school was widely considered to be more of an academically challenging institution than the average local public school. I was about to become the first African-American to graduate from that high school.

Enter Charlene.

Charlene transferred to our school during our senior year and we were instructed to welcome her with open arms. Most of the students graduating from my class had transferred from the other Christian school I attended while in 7th and 8th grade. Charlene was cool and we all liked her, including me. She and I talked frequently. I liked her because she made good grades and I could tell she was more comfortable with me than the rest of my classmates. One day, she told me a bit of her story.

Charlene had always dreamed of attending a Christian school. One of the other students told me that the financial demands were just too great for her family. Sometime before Christmas (I think) she transferred over. She had been given a scholarship to attend. We didn't talk every day, but when we did it was always a meaningful and heartfelt conversation. We often talked about God and I knew she took her relationship with Jesus seriously. I liked her. We were friends.

In the last couple of weeks leading up to graduation, the administrators called us both into the office. The administrators told us both to prepare a speech because based on the last four years of school, she was named valedictorian and I was to be named salutatorian. I was stunned. I tried not to show it in front of my friend.

Charlie was all smiles and she appropriately congratulated me. I congratulated her as well. I assumed she knew I was a bit disappointed, but I'm sure she didn't know why.

I thought about this day after day. I became stoic and depressed. I couldn't figure out how someone could transfer into a school halfway through their senior year and still be awarded valedictorian. She had not faced the academic rigors of any of her new peers. I didn't understand, but then again I did. At that point, all I wanted to do was get out of that school and away from those people. Truth was, I had enough credits to graduate at Christmas time. Some of my classmates were in the same academic position and they left school early to work part time jobs. I hung around just to play basketball.

I was expected to give a moving speech that honored God, family, and the Christian institution I was graduating from. I prepared a very different speech; however, once again I could not match my vindictive intentions with anything in the word of God, so I relented. I honestly don't remember what I said. What I remember most about graduation day was

that my mother gave me the most wonderful card I'd ever received up to that point in my life and that made the day better. I also remember cutting out a picture that looked something like this (Polyp) (left) out of the newspaper and pasting it in my high school scrapbook.

I remember showing it to Charlene and she seemed disappointed that I felt that way.

A week or two prior to graduation, each of the seniors had to meet with a counselor about our post-graduation plans. This is when things got ridiculous.

The guidance counselor said, "Raymond, I think you should consider going to a Votech school or a trade school." Without cracking a smile, I looked at him and told him I was going to Bob Jones University in the fall. I smiled, rose gracefully from my chair, asked to be excused and left. I decided then and there that I would never speak to him or listen to any more of these teachers for the rest of my life.

Yeah. Bob Jones University. Let's talk about that.

All year long, most of the teachers constantly urged the seniors to prayerfully consider attending Bob Jones – a Christian institution in the south. Several of our teachers graduated from Bob Jones. After a while, it was so heavily advertised and shoved down our throats that it became a running joke - until one very magical moment. You see, my best friend Brian and I found out that the teachers weren't telling us everything...

One day, Brian and I were talking to the world's coolest teacher and Christian. He didn't attend a Christian college. He attended a secular college and was the quarterback on the football team. He also happened to be one of the sports coaches. Every day he told us that he woke up and wanted to die so he could be in the presence of Jesus.

He loved God a whole lot!

After class, we were just hanging around his desk when one of us jokingly told him, "Yeah... you know we want to go to Bob Jones University." He laughed and sarcastically said...

"I'm sure you do, but you know that Ray can't go..."

Brian asked, "Why is that coach?"

"Because he's black, and they don't allow blacks to attend their college..."

Crickets.

At that moment, Brian and I looked at each other with wicked smiles and grinchy-grins. We'd just won the "in your face" lottery.

We practically sprinted out of his classroom and ran to find the first teacher we could who attended that school. We ran into the home economics teacher first. With a straight face I looked at her and said, "After prayerfully considering my options, I've decided to take your advice and attend Bob Jones University in the fall."

The blood drained from her face.

"Would you help me get in?" I asked.

Brian could no longer hold it in. He burst out laughing. I laughed so hard I cried. The teacher was a red-faced, hysterical mess. She pulled Brian aside and tried to scold him. Brian was having none of it. He couldn't begin to understand the gross duplicity of Christian racism. You never saw me without Brian or Brian without me.

Before 1971, African Americans could not attend Bob Jones University. By the time I graduated from high school, they would only admit black students if they were married. They had instituted a ban on interracial dating, which of course could not be substantiated by scripture. This remained their policy until March of 2000.[5] (Statement about Race at BJU, 2015)

---

[5] For almost two centuries American Christianity, including BJU in its early stages, was characterized by the segregationist ethos of American culture. Consequently, for far too long, we allowed institutional policies regarding race to be shaped more directly by that ethos than by the principles and precepts of the Scriptures. We conformed to the culture rather than providing a clear Christian counterpoint to it. In so doing, we failed to accurately represent the Lord and to fulfill the commandment to love others as ourselves. For these failures we are profoundly sorry. Though no known antagonism toward minorities or expressions of racism on a personal level have ever been tolerated on our campus, we allowed institutional policies to remain in place that were racially hurtful. On national television in March 2000, Bob Jones III, who was the university's president until 2005, stated that BJU was wrong in not admitting African-American students before 1971, which sadly was a common practice of both public and private universities in the years prior to that time. On the same program, he announced the lifting of the University's policy against interracial dating.

The Final Move

This was the world I lived in. When I tell people my story, they don't understand why I don't hate white people and why I don't hate God. I hate racism. For a time, I hated all racist people no matter what they looked like. But most of all I hated organized religion. Anything that didn't have to do with having a personal relationship with Jesus Christ was of no use to me.

By complete accident, I *thought* I'd found a way to keep the wolves at bay and a way to get people to like me. In reality, all I managed to do was get them to leave me alone.

They left me alone because I helped our team win games. They left me alone because I was smart and made good grades. I was their poster child for Christianity – I was clearly one of the spiritual leaders at the schools. But the joke was still on me; I thought that they liked me because of all of the things I was doing right.

They did not.

All I managed to do was to keep the wolves at bay.

The Raven and the Monster

Unfortunately I rejected some of the advice I should have listened to.

As I said before, there were a couple of teachers who did not practice racism or classism. One of these teachers had been watching me for almost two years.

At the start of my junior year, I went to a church service where they talked about soul-winning. I wanted to be obedient, so I signed up to go out with the group the next week.

I assumed that I would be trained on how to do it, so I went thinking I would just sit back and learn.

They taught us the "Romans Road" method of evangelism, divided us into teams and immediately sent us out into the streets to win souls. Since I was one of the oldest students there, they made me a team leader. I was scared to no end. I remember thinking that I could not do it. At that very moment, they told the groups that we were just being obedient and that God was the one who would do the work of salvation – that we were just messengers. The assured me that I was correct; I could not do it. They reminded me that God alone was the one who could change a life and save a soul. They drove us to our block and dropped us off. The younger kids let me do all the talking. I don't remember how I got through it, but the first young lady we spoke to wanted Jesus in spite of me stumbling through the plan of salvation. That day we led two people to the Lord. I was hooked and I felt like I finally understood what being a Christian was all about. I went out every chance I got.

I continued to go out during both my junior and senior years. At the start of my last year of high school when we elected officers, every one voted for me to be the class chaplain. On one hand, I represented Christ to the world and the unsaved, and all the other hand *I defied* the school's leadership.

At the end of the year, a group of teachers approached me about going to Bible College and eventually going into the ministry. One of the teachers looked and me and said, "You can reach people that we could never reach. We want you to minister to the people in the black community."

They were right. Right about my calling and about what my next steps should have been but all I could think about was the following two things:

1) All preachers I know are poor, and
2) I can't trust *you people* – you just told me I should go to trade school. Why would I ever take your advice about something as important as ministry and the rest of my life?

Besides, I was still sold on the idea of playing basketball. Unfortunately, during that season of my life, I did not know or understand the Golden

Rule of sports, which is:

"If no one is asking you to play for them, your career is over. Period."

The awards I won in high school were more of a testimony of God's fulfillment of Psalms 37:4 in my life[6]. They were not a testimony of my talents.

I was just not that good. At the height of my game, I was at best an average Division II player. When I graduated from high school, I was not at the height of my game, I couldn't shoot very well and I definitely could not dribble. When you are only 5'11" with limited skills, it's a basketball death sentence. No one was scouting me and no one wanted to give me a scholarship. I tried out for the local Juco team and promptly got cut, but I didn't give up — the dream would not die that easily.

I played competitively for the next four years in the Air Force and then took my place in the ranks of the weekend and Saturday morning legends. More about that later.

I now realize that their proposal deserved more consideration that I gave it. I honestly wish they had the wisdom and presence of mind to have this chat with me while my parents were present.

The fact that I decided to be bitter after all the good that God did for me that year still shocks me. I took my eyes off God and focused on my pain.

---

[6] Delight thyself also in the LORD: and he shall give thee the desires of thine heart.

This was not a good idea.

Nevermore

I absolutely love the poem, "The Raven" by Edgar Allen Poe. Although Poe never intended for his poem to be allegorical or didactic, I certainly gave it a great deal of thought and tried to draw some conclusions and life lessons from it. When I'd considered my recent experiences, I reasoned that my "Lenore" was racism and elitism. Was it destined to scar me and stay with me forever? Nevermore. Could I just sweep the experience under the rug and pretend that it never happened? Nevermore. And so my struggles began…

I would not allow myself to fall prey to racist behavior – I did not want to become a victim of my own experiences. But I did make a vow to myself never to let anyone verbally or physically abuse me again. Nevermore.

So I turned to my orange friend and my own people, but they both rejected me as well.

I graduated from high school in 1977. I enrolled in college in the fall of the same year at Kansas City Community Junior College.

College was a much more diverse setting. I walked around the campus and smiled – I saw black people.   But by then, I was too different. Not on all levels, but I was different enough to be the object of ridicule and laughter.   Nothing malicious, but once again I was an outsider.   I constantly got questions like, "Why do you have to study all the time?" "Why don't you come to our parties?" "You went to school...where?" "Why are you friends with 'those people'?" I slowly started to fit in, but it cost me.

After I joined the Air Force, I played on the base basketball team, but that was just a time waster and a leftover residual from my attempts to self-medicate my wounds and to feel better about myself.   At least there were no more racist Christians - and that was good enough for me. Anything was better than my junior high and high school experiences. I wasn't sure of who I was and what I wanted to be – but life was definitely getting better.

This whole post-Christian school era was filled with new experiences and...new declarations. A whole list of "nevermores" filled my psyche, my vocabulary and my life. I personally have learned that it is not a good idea to make declarations like this when you have not healed from whatever it is that has you locked up. Now my pain was forcing me to uphold and enforce a new set of rules to live by. I now realize that I was allowing the people who were responsible for the events that happened during those six years to control my life and destiny even though they were hundreds of miles away.

I created a lot of work that my soul was going to have to undo in the future version of myself. Nevermore.

The Birth of a Monster

It occurred to me that during this pivotal time, my general approach to life was to turn my back on everything I'd been taught. I was anxious to be accepted by my new African American community even though it was obvious that I was going to have to make some compromises. This was not necessarily because they were black, it was just because they were not following the same teachings of Christ that I was accustomed to. Unfortunately, I'd associated everything Christian with the negative aspects of the racist/elitist culture I'd just escaped. I'd just tossed the baby out with the bath water.

That turned out to be a recipe for disaster.

I mixed this new-found attitude with a drive to succeed at any costs. This meant that I'd do almost anything to reach my goals and fulfill my desires. Outside of a Christian environment and without a God-given vision for my life, my desires grew darker and my goals became more and more self-serving and self-centered. I could sense myself becoming heartless and ruthless. As a Christian, people were supposed to be my #1 priority. The condition of their souls and their overall well-being should have been at the forefront of my thoughts and plans. Unfortunately, my success and my well-being became my #1 goals.

I was driven and unstoppable. I started using my gifts to serve my new god...ME!

I was taking on new bad habits almost weekly and directing my own life. I had turned into a monster.

June 27, 1978 – Running Away

As I mentioned earlier, even though I now was in a more diverse setting, I still felt like an outsider. I did; however, realize that I didn't fit in with any other group of people either. I was stuck in the middle. I was not too different, but I was one-off on enough levels for the persecution to turn into mild ridicule and laughter. In some respects, college was kind of the same, but different enough not to cry foul. I had a lot of questions to answer, but eventually I began to fit in. In the end, it would cost me.

The process of fitting in involved me compromising my standards and filling the hole in my soul with academics and the occasional thrill of a pickup basketball game on the weekends.

There was only one problem.

I no longer had an enemy to fight. No more monsters chasing me. I was in the ring shadowboxing.

I was living my life on autopilot. My old enemy "racism" had me right where it wanted me. What happened next can only be described as, "the years of self-destruction."

Were my days of dealing with racism over? Hardly. But the days of constant torment and abuse were done. Like a warrior without a war to fight or a runner without a race to run, I wandered about poised for some kind of action. I was like a bullet shot from a gun that had no target – I was going nowhere fast and I was destined to be the cause of an innocent bystander getting hurt.

My new non-Christian friends had an easy time persuading me to join them in whatever they had going on. That "whatever" attitude led me to make the decision to follow two of my friends into the United States Air Force. I refer to this as "Plan B."

I remember coming home and sitting at the kitchen table with my father. I had on my yellow see-thru muscle shirt. I don't think he knew what I wanted to say to him. I was a little afraid to tell him about my plans because I was pretty sure I knew he would disapprove. It was the first time I would go against my father's wishes and advice. There was only one other time, but both incidents would lead to years of destruction and wasted time while I desperately tried to recover from my short-sighted disobedience.

"Well son," my father replied, "You are a man now. If that is what you want to do, go ahead."

So on June 27th, 1978, I raised my right hand and took the oath of enlistment. Not a bad decision, all things considered. But it's important to remember that I was carrying around the package that racism had left at my doorstep. It's hard to get where you need to go with an albatross around your neck.

"Can bitter and sweet water both flow from the same fountain?"[7] Being in the military with a hole in your soul and a chip on your shoulder is a bad combination – trouble was looking for me and I was looking for it. It took almost a year before I set foot in another church. I didn't really harbor any ill will towards white people but I did start to notice the stereotypes they ascribed to me and I decided that I didn't like them. I was determined to vocally object and prove to them that they were wrong about me and others that looked like me. Later, I realized that this became my own self-inflicted prison. Unwittingly, I had given *people* control of my actions. More than likely, they probably could have cared less about my overall well-being. Not that they were out to get me, they just though what they thought and the content of their prejudices and stereotypes shouldn't have mattered that much to me. I was still trying to prove myself worthy of their acceptance; if it wasn't with basketball or intellect, it was usually with some other over-the-top, demonstrative behavior.

The slippery slope is the "acceptance" part. It wasn't until years later that I realize that one should never have to earn racial acceptance because it almost never happens. If you meet someone and they are truly dead-set against giving you a fair shake, your efforts to prove your worth or worthiness will almost always be rejected. In most cases, you are facing a formidable foe in the form of a lifetime of environmental programming and experiential hardwiring. Even if you turn the tide, the investment is

---

[7] James 3:11 (KJV)

rarely worth it. I still have yet to gain a true friend from this type of effort. Usually, you end up reinforcing their beliefs in exactly why they don't like you.

I was not the type of person that needed to be in a super-structured environment like the Air Force where creative thinking was not encouraged. I stuck out like a sore thumb because I was more of a forward thinker. Thankfully, I understood obedience and authority, so I would always comply, but only after I'd challenged the rules and the status-quo.

There are benefits to serving in the military. A person can gain valuable experience and benefit from the discipline the service demands. These are assets that will aid anyone throughout life's journey. *Fortunately*, my parents and grandparents had already instilled these character traits in me and my siblings. *Unfortunately*, it did not prevent me from getting into things I shouldn't have. By the time I got out of the Air Force I'd been married and divorced and developed a horrible temper. I was suffering from a broken heart and I had an Article 15 (non-judicial punishment) on my record. Despite going to college for most of my 2 tours of duty, I still did not have a degree but I did have 4 years of computer programming experience after my 8 years were finished. Had I stayed at home, I would have completed college in 4 years and I still would have had 4 years of experience. Most likely I would have been farther ahead in life. I was blessed with a daughter from my marriage, but she was taken from me in a bizarre set of circumstances. Although I got custody of her after I was discharged, I had to face the fact that my mistakes were beginning to hurt other people.

Hurting people hurt people and I was doing that in spades.

God did get me back on track. I got involved in soul-winning again. While I was helping others to get saved, God was saving me – from myself. I also started singing in the choir, but mostly I showed up to play the part of the clown, tell jokes and to be an overall distraction to everyone. I always had to be the center of attention.

One day I showed up and the music director told us that we would be hosting a workshop and a musical. Several musicians showed up to help us. One guy played the saxophone.

I thought to myself...I can do that...

After the musical, I drove back home to K.C. and dug my old saxophone out of the back of the closet where I'd left it after my last band practice in high school. I brought it back to Oklahoma and started practicing like a man possessed. Initially, played just to have something new to do – some other accomplishment and skill to chase after. I wanted to be just like my cousin. He was a recording artist. He was fairly well-known and everybody liked him. That sounded good to me.

One night, I had trouble sleeping – and I never have trouble sleeping. After a couple of hours of restlessness, I got up and I had the distinct impression that I should ask God what He wanted from me. I remember recalling the story of young Samuel hearing God call out to him at night and somehow, this seemed strangely familiar. I never heard anything audible, but I definitely felt impressed to "do something." For two nights in a row, I didn't sleep well. Since I was playing a horn, I interpreted this message to mean that God wanted me to be a saxophonist. I made an appointment to talk to my pastor. After telling him everything that happened, he said an interesting thing. He told me, "I think you are confusing what you heard with a call of God for you to be in the ministry." And I said,

"No. I am not..."

I can't think of a more pompous, arrogant and narcissistic thing to say to someone who was supposed to be my spiritual leader and guide. What made me think that I was qualified to interpret what God was telling me? I had no history of spiritual experience in this area, and I certainly was not emotionally and psychologically stable.

So he did a wise thing. He told me to start praying more and to get serious about playing. I think that he knew that if I prayed more, I'd get more clarity on what God was wanting me to do with my life.

That was the second time I told God "no" about ministry. They have an old saying that goes something like this, "Stop running from God." I never felt like I was running – I always felt like I was meant to have an impact, just not in an official ministry capacity. The issue was not whether or not I was hearing correctly, it was that my heart was not receptive to doing anything but what I wanted to do. God can correct our life's course if we are open do doing what He commands. I was not open.

In the meantime, somewhere at the same time and in the same geographical area, my current Pastor was saying "Yes" to God and the call.

I think I was up to plan "C" by now. Playing my horn actually kept me coming to church, although initially my motives were not right or pure. My playing was undeniably a blessing to others, but I secretly loved hearing people tell me how well I played and how good I sounded. My friend Lee told me that he thought that I took on an alternate personality when I played. He was right! As I matured, things would change and so would my motives. I don't know if I would have ever picked up my horn if I were back home in Kansas City. In some ways, joining the service was a direct catalyst for me becoming a serious musician.

So what was I doing while I was out of position? I was running from my feelings and layering my hurt with things that made me feel good about myself like pursuing intellect, women, basketball, music, and engaging in over the top behavior. At this point in my life, I am no longer pursuing these things. For the first time in my journey, I have a real opportunity to pursue God and to figure out who I really am.

Back then, my life had no real direction except to pursue success and to make myself feel ok.

The Final Move

For almost 8 years, I practiced religion but my true god was me.

How could I end up so far away from where I was supposed to be? Until I was willing to face the monster, I would continue to be controlled by it. As I grew older and bolder, I discovered that one way I could keep people from hurting me was to use my fists and loud voice to control people and situations. Sometimes it worked and sometimes it backfired. More than anything, it grew tiring and if you ask me, I quit doing in just the nick of time. There were just too many stupid things happening in my life – I was fighting and threating people. I pulled a gun on another airman. I would verbally challenge people in traffic. My time in the service was a very sad time in retrospect. There was nothing wrong with the service, I just had no business being there. For me, the Air Force was my trip to Tarshish instead of going to Nineveh.[8]

I have heard a lot of people tell their stories – stories about how their upbringing and environment lead to them make bad choices. I never liked people who made excuses for their bad behavior, so I never did. I discounted my past and took responsibility for my shortcomings, but it didn't change anything. I kept making one bad decision after another.

I also started making negative confessions. I saw how my life was going. Somewhere around the age of 25, I started telling my friends that I didn't think I would live to see age 30. I often sang a song to myself during this time of my life,

---

[8] The story of Jonah and the Great Fish details his unwillingness to go where God sent him. Because he was out of position, he wound up in the belly of a fish for 3 days and nights.

"Don't let the sun, go down on me. Although I search myself, it's always someone else I see..." (John & Taupin, 1975)

I passionately sang these words because I knew I was running out of time to make a real impact with my life and I knew that I really didn't know who I was. I knew what I wanted to do, but that was based on my worldly view of success and happiness. But I would press on, me and my indomitable, wild and irrepressible spirit.

Somehow by grace, my obligation to Uncle Sam ended without me going to jail and I got out of the military with an honorable discharge. Although God has an amazing way of getting something out of our messes, anyone with any kind of spiritual sensitivity could hear, "tick, tock goes the clock...Ray is wasting precious time."

A Stick to Beat Me With

But every man is tempted, when he is drawn away of his own lust, and enticed. *(James 1:14)*

I do not forget any good deed done to me & I do not carry a grudge for a bad one. *(Frankl, 1946)*

Everyone knows someone that is widely regarded as a crazy person. We are quick to jump to the conclusion that these people act that way because they think that they are normal and don't know that they are...different. During still, solitude moments, I believe that every person who fits this description comes to the realization that something is wrong. I believe they realize that the way they are thinking and acting cannot be justified and at the end of the day, the coping mechanisms are just a way for them to feel better about themselves. When you get to that place in time, you want to change – change your life and how you act. I know that's how I felt.

I hadn't traced my aberrant behavior back to racism, but I did want to stop acting in a way that was not socially acceptable.

Well, too bad, Ray. That's not how the deal works.

At first, I seemed to be in control of my habits, but the longer I indulged in them, the more the habits started to take a hold of me. Soon they turned in to a big stick that I routinely used to beat myself with. There is no worse feeling in the world than to want to quit doing something and not have the power to do it. Each failure to overcome made me feel like a loser. Suddenly I realized that I was no longer the one in control.

The biggest problem with racism and hatred is that you cannot contain it. First, you hate whatever it is you hate. Soon the hatred can no longer be contained and you start to hate everyone who doesn't share your hatred. Ultimately, you end up hating yourself. And whether or not I was willing to admit it, I did not like myself.

Life for me was tough enough without developing habits that made it even tougher.

Racism destroys in more than one way. The recipient of the hate can take on a posture of revenge and retaliation. This is not the position of a winner. Combine this with all of the other baggage I'd managed to accumulate and you can see that I was headed nowhere fast. Instead of trying to avoid conflict and trouble, I was now looking for it. I woke up each morning looking for a fight and anxious to get into some kind of mischief.

I've discovered that emotional wounds don't just go away. Like their physical counterparts, these untreated wounds leave ugly scars. The more serious my wounds were, the more I became infected. Some of my injuries left behind deformities.

This is important for parents to understand. If you cannot correctly assess your child's emotional development or response to a particular environment, you must accept the fact that your child will become one of the walking wounded.

I had gaping emotional wounds. They were un-kept, untreated and they definitely turned into deformities. The farther away I got from the actual abuse, the easier it became to ignore and mask the pain. It was always there and would sometimes manifest itself in crude conduct, the need to prove myself to others, narcissistic behavior, sexual misconduct and low-self-esteem. Every goal and undertaking was rooted in pleasing or trying to please and impress others. It is shocking to think how many actions in my life were affected by my emotional instability. Despite my parent's best efforts, I did not possess the inner strength at that age (seventh grade) to endure persecution. All of the tools and weapons for self-preservation were present and at my disposal; that being the Word of God and my understanding of black culture and history; however, I did not have the strength to wield them.

By now, my pain and problems were so far removed and buried so deeply that I began to question my sanity. Why was I acting this way?

The thing that made this so hard to figure out is that on the surface, I was a likeable and successful guy. The only people who knew I had "issues" were the people who knew me personally. On the surface, I had a good job, money and talent. In case you didn't know, money and success is the difference between being called eccentric as opposed to being called crazy.

This was the other side of my coin. The drive to succeed and to prove that I belonged at the table was the very thing that was the primary contributor to my success. I still wanted to prove my worthiness, but not because I was being racially oppressed. Racism was still alive, but it was less stressful if not for the simple fact that no one was trying to beat me up every day or call me names...to my face.

Each day, the curtains lifted after about 6:00 pm and the specter of my personal life came out like a vampire at night...

...and I would pick up my stick and beat myself with it. I wanted to quit. I wanted to stop the attention-getting behavior. I tried to ignore the head shakes and negative looks – I tried hard to pretend that they didn't matter. I wanted to be normal and I wanted to fit in with the others but I just couldn't fight off the bad habits, the voices and the urges.

My biggest regret is time. All of the wasted time and years. I feel as though my instability caused me to chase after every shiny thing I saw. I've wanted to be a preacher, a doctor, an accountant, a businessman, a gospel sax recording artist, a technologist, a husband and a father. Along the way, I took the time and effort to become proficient at chess, music, cooking, pool and table tennis (just to name a few). I just never got focused.

In the end, the only two things that have endured the test of time are my love for God and my love for music.

All Grown Up (Now I'm Better)

But grow in grace, and in the knowledge of our Lord and
Saviour Jesus Christ. To him be glory both now and forever.
Amen. *(2 Peter 3:18)*

It is not freedom from conditions, but it is freedom to take a
stand toward the conditions. *(Frankl, 1946)*

Some of my problems vanished once the actors called age and maturity showed up on the stage of my life. Most of these changes in behavior were required *by my job* in order for me to *do my job*. In that respect, I was coerced into compliance. Each time I'd land a job with more responsibility, I would just happen to find a mentor who would help me to grow up a little more. Similarly, each time I found a new church, I'd leave a little more chaos behind. Up to that point, my life was symbolic of a wild party with wild friends (bad habits) who came to my house, ate up my food, drained my resources and left the place a wreck. In the end, it was my responsibility to clean up the place and replenish everything – why? Because I was the one who initiated the party and invited in all the mayhem. The work was slow going; each time I thought that the place was cleaned up, I'd find some trash in an obscure place in a corner or under the cushions of my sofa. What a life and what a chore!

I'd be remiss if I didn't mention how my journey was deeply affected by my growing exploration of my relationship with God. The more the years rolled by, the more I learned and discovered who I was and my purpose in life. I'm not talking about practicing religion, in fact, I've proven over the years to be quite clueless when it comes to being fluent in the area of church policies and politics. Plainly stated, my life is an accumulation of triumphs, failures, grace and mercy, correction and special times when I knew that I was experiencing God's intervention on my behalf. I was experiencing what it was like to be in a healthy relationship!

I learned what freedom meant – I learned that I did not have to be a slave to my passions and my cravings. I learned how not to give into them. None of this happened until I could admit that part of me did not want to get too close to God for fear that He would ask, prompt or lead me to do something I did not want to do or to become someone I did not want to be. Once I finally got the revelation straight in my head, that is, the revelation that He had my best interests in mind; the desire to pursue only my happiness and success became less of a struggle for me. In fact, the core and source of my awakening and healing is that *I have the proper perspective of my misfortunes, stresses, and struggles.* Understanding these difficult parts of my life's journey made it easier for me to accept my purpose. Knowing that I was not a victim of constant misfortune or anything else allowed me to grow and become stronger. It allowed me to grow into my purpose and the reason I was born.

At some point in a boxer's career he or she is going to have to learn how to take a punch, get up off the canvas, regain a clear head and survive the round. I don't know about you, but knowing that I can take a hit and keep going is a source of strength. I know that those hits served a purpose and propelled me to my destiny. Knowing that makes the journey worthwhile. It made realize that my life had meaning and it brought my meaningless suffering to an end.

A Kinder, Gentler Racism – Corporate America

An abnormal reaction to an abnormal situation is normal
behavior. *(Frankl, 1946)*

Corporate America is the ultimate proving ground for individuals who have either paid their dues in college or accumulated enough equivalent experience. They have not only learned the art of their profession, but the skill of professionalism. Professionalism in the corporate world requires mastering the nuances of a dress code, work ethic, and a certain set of language skills – both verbal and written. As you go higher, you have to be skilled at working across organizational lines and understanding the politics of getting ahead and getting things done.

It's tough for a person who may have come from a blue collar setting to make the shift to corporate life; it's like running a gauntlet. The differences are stark and shocking. In some ways, working in a blue collar profession is a bit refreshing – at least you know who your enemies are.

People talked about a corporate glass ceiling but as I began to pay closer attention, I noticed that they were letting a few of "us" trickle through. Watching all of this from a front row seat made me ask, "Why did *that person* get to go to the big dance?" "What are they doing to make it happen?" At that time in my life, I could only get an answer to one of those questions.

At the time, most successful minorities were surviving and existing by trial and error. Why? Because there were no accessible mentors at the levels we were all aiming for on the corporate side. The entrepreneurial side was a different matter.

Two of the most successful African American businessmen in Kansas City were my relatives; my father and my uncle. They were part of a cadre of businessmen that experienced a great deal of success in the late 1970's by successfully navigating the government's 8(a) minority program.[9] My uncle forged an alliance with Mr. Leroy Tombs and my father's first foray into entrepreneurial business was a partnership with my uncle called, "The Rib Shack." It was a wildly successful and popular barbeque restaurant in the newly developed Indian Springs Shopping Mall. I was 13 years old at the time and I had a front row seat when it came to learning about business.

The racism that my father and uncle faced was unbelievable. I am just now able to piece together all of the stories. The mall ownership tried several different strategies to shut down the restaurant; everything from calling the health department to attempting to impose fire code and insurance restrictions on them. There were always issues to deal with.

---

[9] The 8(a) Business Development Program helps small, disadvantaged businesses compete in the marketplace.

The fun parts were really fun. I noticed the difference in our family's lifestyle right away. Nothing overly ostentatious, but a noticeable change in status. We were living in a new home. My sister and I started attending private Christian school. My dad was the best I'd ever seen when it came to overseeing finances and investments. I remember my father helping me to understand the stock market when I was in 8th grade. I picked my stocks and kept track of my "portfolio." I'm glad I was using fake money!

The restaurant brought in a lot of celebrities and dignitaries. There was always a long line of customers that trailed out of the restaurant and down the main promenade of the mall. This was problematic because it made it difficult for customers trying to patronize the other merchant's shops near us. This only added to the growing list of people who wanted us out of the mall. Some were jealous, some were prejudiced and some were just concerned about their own investment failing due to all of the chaos.

Even with all of the controversy, The Rib Shack was making money hand over fist. Most of the workers were a part of our extended family – it was a family business.

Every weekend I helped out – mostly as a dishwasher. I had explicit instructions to stay in the back of the restaurant and out of sight. Being in the back did not stop me from watching and observing how a business worked. I learned all about customer service, profits and supply chain from my vantage point in the kitchen. I also saw how trust could be extended and violated.

A lot of the family saw this business venture as a way out of their situation – whatever it was. Some were hard working and saw the potential of it becoming something big. Some didn't. Some felt that the restaurant was something that could be exploited and could help feed their families. Things for me started to decline when they caught my cousin stealing money out of another employee's purse. That spelled the end of under-aged kids getting the opportunity to work in the restaurant. I understand that the final nail in the coffin was due to "internal misappropriation of funds." With all of the cost-cutting measures my dad did to try and keep things afloat, once the business could not pay its quarterly taxes, the end was inevitable. Both my dad and uncle were upset over "something" that a family member did that was connected to the finances and the demise of the Rib Shack. In this case, racism didn't have anything to do with the outcome – it was us. The whole thing would be a strong teaching moment for me.

Racism was a way of life in the 1970's for black business owners. I saw some of what I experienced at Christian school in the business world. It helped me deal with what I was about to face in the corporate world later in life.

While serving my first tour of duty in the Air Force, I would get a taste of the life I was about to experience while making my first transition from working hard with my hands to working with my mind.

One morning, I was sitting at my graphics station at a squadron called "Southern Communications" or "South Comm" for short. It was not too far from the Oklahoma City Air Logistics Command Center. This was (and probably still is), the largest depot repair complex for military aircraft. I knew that my life was not headed in the direction I'd planned. I had a list of personal problems I was dealing with that had directly derailed my master plan of going to school and completing my degree while working in the computer programming field. I was in a failing marriage, still playing basketball everyday (wasting time), playing the church game each Sunday and I was working in a job field that I hated. There was nothing wrong with the graphics field, it just wasn't what I wanted. So I decided that this would be the day I would take action to end the madness.

That afternoon, I wandered over to the other side of the airbase and to big, gray brick building next to the AWAC Squadron. I parked across the street where I could still see the tops of the rotor domes on the E3A airplanes. This building was a windowless fortress of locked doors. When I asked people passing by whether or not it was the computer programming center, all I got was blank stares. I didn't really know who I needed to talk to but I went across the street and knocked on what I thought was the front door.

I was desperate to get out of my situation and I knew if I didn't do something different, I'd end up staying in the military and I had already surmised that it was not the kind of life I was destined to live.

I knocked for 20 minutes.

I didn't realize I was knocking on an access door to get to yet another door that let you into a very noisy computer center. This was a place with hundreds of computers housed on raised flooring in a temperature controlled and extremely noisy room. The chances of someone hearing me knock were a thousand to one. This single event encapsulated in that 20 minutes redefined my life and changed my destiny.

The door opened and a Chief Master Sargent was staring me in the face. He looked familiar.

"You're Jarrett, right?"

"Yes, sir."

"Don't call me sir...I work for a living, son."

"Yes, Chief."

"What can I do for you son?"

"I want to work here Chief. I took programming classes in college and I will do whatever it takes to work here."

"Wow, I'm impressed. Come in and I will see what I can do to help you. You were really a sharp troop in there a couple of months ago."

I'd met CMS Jim Cerney at the below-the-zone (BTZ) competition. BTZ was an opportunity for E-3s to get promoted to E-4 up to a year ahead of schedule. I was one of a handful of successful candidates and had already been notified that I was getting promoted. Chief Cerney was one of the panelists on the selection board.

So far, so good.

The Chief laid out a possible plan and path for me to reach my goal. He pulled a few strings to pull it together but in the end, it would be all up to me. I would have to do almost 18 months of "stuff" to become a programmer. There were lots of twists and turns and there were many opportunities for me to quit. In the end, I finished programming school and all of my other prerequisites. After graduation from school, I got orders cut for me to transfer to the AFCCPC SOCR/OCR group. I was in!!!

There are a million unwritten rules to learn when you are adjusting to working in an office setting, particularly when there are politics involved. You have to know that it is considered grossly unprofessional to take personal calls at work, especially ones that last more than a minute or two. You need to know that it is considered poor form to take all of your sick days – if you are not sick. The whole, "just because they are mine" mindset is considered unprofessional. I quickly learned that they were more like having insurance – they were there if you needed them. You have to learn that it is considered poor form to not work *some* overtime. You need to know that you should never, ever come to work late. If you are not 15 minutes early, you are late. 30 minutes early is better. You need to have reliable transportation that doesn't smoke or leak. Most of the other professionals will make up their minds about you and your work ethic – permanently – in about 60 days. After that, you will be able to do no wrong or do no right.

Do you like loud clothes? Bright colors? Flamboyant shoes, nails and hairstyles? If so, please report to the mailroom. Do not pass GO and do not collect $200.00. There is nothing wrong with that style, but you will never make it in the corporate world dressing that way. Remember, it's never cool to borrow money. Co-workers are just that – they are not really your friends so don't spill your guts to them at work.

I could fill this book with hundreds of these unwritten rules but the basic overall strategy is not to do anything to stick out, but to do enough extra to stand out and get noticed. If you are a minority, you have to know that you will have to work harder than everyone else to accomplish your goals. You will also need to know the difference between being treated differently because of your race and being treated differently because you didn't know the rules of the game.

I know what you might be thinking...and the answer is "No."

No one is going to pull you aside and tell you any of this stuff. No one is going to tell you if you are blowing it. You will need to ask questions and you will need a mentor. The rules vary from company to company. You need to let yourself be assimilated by the collective. Some of you will understand this reference!

In that respect, the Air Force was the perfect place for me because it was a great training ground for a green professional who'd never had a thinking, desk job. I was immature and I had personal problems. The military didn't give a hoot about me being black but I could not tell the difference because elitism (I'm better and smarter than you) and classism (I'm better and richer than you), look a lot like racism (I'm better than you because I don't look like you). They certainly all leave you with the same feeling. You feel like a zero.

I vacillated back and forth between feeling like I was being discriminated against and feeling ostracized. I was a green, rookie programmer but instead realizing that they were just better programmers than I was because they'd been at it longer, I took their comments and their overall approach towards me to mean that they felt as though they were smarter than I was. If I had gone with the "you've done this longer than I have" mindset, I could have gleaned from their experience instead of feeling like I had to do everything on my own. As I stated earlier, nothing set me off quicker than for someone to assume that I was not intelligent – for any reason.

I nearly blew it. I had many problems. I had car problems. Marital problems. I couldn't focus. I didn't know the value of taking work home or studying my craft on my own time. My attention was still partly on basketball. And to top it all off, I let my temper get me in trouble by overreacting to my marital issues. All of these thing added up to me being "that guy" and it made me get noticed for all of the wrong reasons.

Thankfully, my first enlistment came to an end. I stopped wasting my time trying to prove that I was the best basketball player alive and went back to college to get my degree in computer science. I purchased a good running car and I stopped acting so needy. I stopped wearing weird hairdos and I stopped leaving work at exactly quitting time. I got out of the Air Force and started working for Oklahoma Teaching Hospitals as a Tech Specialist. But, I was still a little wet behind the ears.

Corporate America is like being in a pack of dogs. You can be a cat, but you are going to stick out like a sore thumb. It's not that you are bad, you are just very different. This means that when there are two people of equal talent and there is only one promotion to hand out, the dog will get the promotion every time.

Some of the black people I have worked with would get wind of the rules and the politics and subsequently label the whole set of practices under the category of "not being real." They saw the whole system as a reason to distrust people. They didn't realize that that they were being left out because they would not play by the rules. I was a staunch member of this little group of dissidents. No one was trying to force me to play golf but golf is one of the accepted games of business professionals. Basketball is not on that list. Going to lunch with a diverse crowd of people is a practice you have to get comfortable with. Refusing to have an open mindset makes you a cat in a dog's world...

...but more importantly it gives the people who are truly prejudice an excuse to overlook you and sweep you under the rug – and the glass ceiling.

I did eventually learn the rules of the game and just like in the game of basketball, if you can't play, people who can play won't pass you the ball. They don't freeze you out of the game because of how you look, they freeze you out because you can't play the game.

Dude, you have no skills!

At Oklahoma Teaching Hospitals, I learned the game. I got some skills.

A big shout out to Rick McDaniel. Rick – you 'da man. And yes, I threw away the pink knit tie and the pastel jacket. Sheesh!!

Now I was ready for some real racism – again.

Cook 'Em like a Frog

No more excuses. It felt good to always be known as the hardest worker in the building. I'd get to work early and I'd stay late. I've been described as a great communicator, a good listener and an excellent presenter. My writing skills are above par level and I am a likeable guy. Most of the people I've worked for have no problem seeing me at higher levels in the organization.

Most, but not all.

Remember, I was still swimming with the sharks at this point in my career. The sharks are smart enough not to call you the n-word to your face. Most of the time they will just let you self-destruct. I call this the "promote and step-back" approach because everyone on the levels above you knows that you are like a ticking time bomb – unless someone comes along to disable you, you're going to blow up! This process takes anywhere from 6 months to a year.

So with all of these variables in play, how could I have possibly known that any type of racism was going on? It seemed that I was going to need a super-hero power to understand the lay of the land. In my case, most of the time my problems weren't personal attacks, they were pervasive, institutional mindsets. Honestly, that kind of behavior was a lot easier to spot.

All I had to do was to look for the biggest organizational tell-tale sign of all. I didn't see anything or anyone at the top level of the organization that resembled the demographics of the workforce and the customers that patronized the business, so I knew I was looking at a place that had some inherent people problems. I saw one or two minorities at the top but they had no skills. This was a dead giveaway and it let me know that the company had no intention of evaluating minorities and women fairly for leadership positions.

I decided that I'd try to change the company I was working at back in the 1990's. Some acquaintances and I decided that we'd get together and form a minority based networking and mentorship program. From a professional and political standpoint, that turned out to be a mistake. Personally, I learned a lot about starting something from nothing. I also learned that an organization is a living entity and will view you in one of two ways; as a vaccine or as a virus.

Most of the other African American associates I knew were at the manager or supervisory level. There were no black directors in the company at that time that I knew of – if so, they were hiding. Our little group had access to demographic data. It showed that our company, was doing fine as far as diversity numbers and percentages. We were lacking when it came to the number of professional / technical people in the organization. Simply put, there were more minorities working in the mail room and driving trucks that there were people in management and in positions of influence. You know that there is a small representation in any demographic when you can look at a graph and name the people represented on the chart. Senior leadership was devoid of anything that resembled diversity.

My friend Rich called me and told me about an idea he had that was designed to create opportunities through mentorships. It was specifically slated for minorities in the organization. I was all in. The amount of work we had to put in was monumental. We had to create a charter, by-laws, stand up local chapters and elect officers to leadership positions. A person in senior leadership from our company's HR department was assigned to us to oversee the process.

All of the professionals who spearheaded the effort truly believed that the corporation was listening and that they were ready to partner with us. They'd financed our coming together and that was no small effort.

We elected our officers. I helped to facilitate the session / discussion on the bylaws. We got to where we wanted to be, and in the end, it was all a huge success!! We were ready to pass the bylaws when someone from the corporate office rose slowly from his seated position at the rear of the room, came forward and made an impassionate speech that went something like this:

"You all are to be commended on your ability to organize around this important cause. A lot of effort has been expended but the company's position is that we cannot allow you to create bylaws or a national charter. You can have...guidelines."

The whole scene was laughable. A hundred or so professionals sat with their mouths agape. We were offered no real reason or explanation. Just – no, can't do it. Of course, there were questions.

But I knew what was happening. And Rich knew.

I rose gracefully from my chair. I had something to say.

"One of the tenants of a successful organization is couched in its ability to organize, assign roles, and to create structure and order. I don't believe we can be effective without this. As you can see, we don't have a subversive agenda. We are simply looking for mentorship."

Crickets.

Another lady rose gracefully. She said, "So does that lighten your load?"

The room erupted with laughter. Our guest was not amused.

"No," he stated emphatically, "You cannot have a national entity nor can you have officers and official bylaws."

When one side of the bargaining table has all of the money and all of the power, there is no real discussion; there can be no real debate or bilateral conversation. One side simply dictates to the other.

The Final Move

So we disbanded. Local chapters only. We couldn't say they told us no. We had all been placed in the proverbial pot of room temperature water. They slowly turned up the heat a little at a time. Less money. No charter. Only a few mentors.

They cooked us alive – the way that you do a frog... And they remembered our faces.

One guy was eventually promoted to director and he is now a vice president at that same company. The rest of us ended up leaving in order to advance our careers.

Did I mention that another unwritten rule is to know when to be quiet? My VP friend didn't say anything that evening. Smart man.

A wonderful thing happened with my career at this point. A good friend of mine called me with an opportunity. He offered me a position at his company as the director of software development. My friend and I both worked for the same company when we were much younger. After leaving that company, he and his dad started their own company and I headed for the safe waters of corporate America. I'd used his software consultants from time to time over the years. Their business niche was software consulting and they'd done very well for themselves over the years. They'd attracted the attention of a large software company and sold it to them. This company was expanding its presence in the KC area and wanted to do in-house software development as well as outsourcing it's consultants.

I got a nice raise and I left the telecommunications company after I sensed it was clear that my upward mobility was now limited. They viewed me as a technician and not a leader.

This new company had a much more relaxed environment and it was characterized by more of an entrepreneurial "let's get things done" attitude. Money did not grow on trees here so you had to be creative to succeed. We did our part for the parent company and we showed some modest growth although their plans for us augmenting their software development efforts in KC never really materialized.

The Final Move

About a year and a half later, we got a call. The parent company was trimming the fat by selling off or closing all of the small acquisitions it had made an attempt to diversify itself. They were going to shut the branch down, or...they would sell the company back to "us." "Us" was some subset of the officers in the company at the local Kansas City office.

In the end, only my friend and I were left standing. After about two months of negotiations, he and I came to an agreement with the parent company. We bought the company back, made some organizational changes, generated some local buzz in the business sector and had a big party. We were going to do it all over again, only bigger this time.

There's much more that goes into the story, but that's not the main point of this part of the tale. After strategizing we came to a remarkable discovery and arrived at a stunning conclusion... we figured out that as a black person, I was a minority and our business qualified for some special privileges. Or so we thought.

I know it sounds ridiculous and even funny but this "realization" happened just that way. We started our research. If we could make the switch to a minority owned business, we would be poised to take advantage of the 8(a) contracting arm of the government. Contracts were waiting on us! Millions in the bank!

Our strategy was simple. We knew we had about one year left on most of our contracts. We had to hire people into our workforce with updated skills or we had to retrain those who were already working for us. In the meantime, we figured it would take 6 to 8 months to get certified and another 3 to 6 months to market ourselves and win contracts. At most, we would have to hold on to half of our current revenue stream for about half a year. On top of that, we had a plan B, plan C, and a Plan D. You get the idea.

Well...

We went to classes, filled out paperwork, assemble a whole binder of paper artifacts and worked hand-in-hand with the SBA office. We spoke to consultants and had people walk us through the process. But all we would get for a response was another request for more information. This went on and on for more than a year. In the 14th month, we were finally turned down because my friend's personal net worth exceeded mine and the SBA officials said that I had not put enough equity into the business. They ignored the fact that I had a controlling interest and that Mike was nowhere near the day-to-day operation of the business.

We asked question after question and presented them with multiple scenarios. In the end, none of it made sense. Quite frankly, I felt as though we were being discriminated against because Mike was white and he had more money than I did.

I was still being affected by racism. It was just in a way I didn't expect. This time, black people were practicing the discriminating behavior and trying to hold me back. At least, it seemed like it was black people, but it could have been some other unknown entity. I'm still not really sure which.

We appealed the decision. We were turned down again. So instead, we tried to qualify as a minority owned business instead of an 8(a) business. That didn't work either.

Too bad for us...

Even though we didn't get any of the certifications we wanted, all of our old customers got wind of what we were trying to do because of our wonderful press releases in the Business Journal. They begin to do a very strange and odd thing. They started reclassify us. You see, most corporations only are required to allocate a certain percentage of business to minority-owned entities. In most cases, the total amount of business we were doing with these corporations already exceeded the "minority allowance." This meant they could reduce the amount of business they were doing with us and give the balance to other companies who were "non-minority."

It seems that it did not pay to be black - both literally and metaphorically.

It's still hard to put into words the enormity of what had transpired over the course of 18 months. Our entire business model hinged on what would seem to be a sure thing – I was a minority running a successful business and I wanted to market myself and business in the segment of the government/state private sector that was supposed to be providing opportunities for corporations like mine.

Since I was the majority shareholder, the banks were looking at my credit in order to make a determination about whether or not they would loan us capital. I still had limited access to capital and opportunities. We wasted considerable time and resources to make this happen.

How could this be possible? The folks at the local office working on our paperwork were baffled.

In the end, my business partner stepped aside so that I could bring in another black business partner. Unfortunately, we ran out of time and money. We tried re-submitting our paperwork and that failed. We tried getting a Hub Zone status and that failed as well.

I was banking on the fact that the world would look at me as a disadvantaged person just one more time. When the chips were on the line, they flipped the script on me.

What our private sector customers did to us was the biggest shock of all. In essence, the rules rewarded them for limiting us to a very small amount of contract dollars. In the end, they were still compliant with government regulations for giving minority and women owned businesses a seat at the table. Essentially, they were telling us how our future was going to turn out and what it was worth.

The Final Move

We would have done better if I'd just kept who I was under wraps and undercover. My black face didn't help us a lick. In fact, it hurt us.

Isn't that a shocking revelation?

We were providing all of the same services at market prices but only got a portion of the overall spend because companies did not have to give us any more money. They did not have to give us any more opportunities. Before all of this, I had companies willing to do business with me based on my firm's capability but now I was being offered a fraction of the contract revenue because that's all their government contract required. I was being offered a piece of the pie all right... A very small piece.

It was enough to make me cuss!

A Look Back and a Look Forward

Ye shall not need to fight in this battle: set yourselves, stand ye still, and see the salvation of the LORD with you... *(2 Chronicles 20:17)*

Between stimulus and response, there is a space. In that space is our power to choose our response. In our response lies our growth and our freedom. *(Frankl, 1946)*

I'm positive that I could not have written this story before now. I wasn't over everything until now. Whenever I'd tell others bits and pieces of my story, they would encourage me to undertake a project like this but I always made excuses. I thought my 8-5 job was more important. I thought my other writing projects were more relevant and worthy of my time. Looking back provides a unique perspective. Wisdom gained by experienced is very, very valuable.

So it gives me great pleasure to pause at this point in my life and offer my perspective and prose on how to escape from the prison of racism.

Before I start this last chapter, I have to say that I know everyone won't feel like my way out – my escape route – is for them. My guess is that most of the people who will feel this way didn't go through what I and others had to endure. They were never trapped by destructive emotions and the collateral damage that imprisons you. Most, if not all people will want to get out of prison anyway they can – by serving their time, by early release, or even by breaking out and escaping.

I'm not saying that there aren't other ways out of this mess. What I am saying is that my way out is the only one I can vouch for. A few months ago, I talked to a young man who'd recently graduated from the same school I attended in junior high. When I told him where I went, his eyes lit up. When I asked them how they treated him he said, "What, like you mean, racism?"

He said it – not me.

I nodded yes. His countenance fell and he told me what I would've told any adult asking me the same question when I was his age.

"It was all good."

I knew he was not ready to confide in me. I told him I'd be around if he ever wanted to talk about it.

My pastor told me about a prominent person in our community who sent his child to an environment where the students were academically challenged. His child was a part of a very small minority of black students. These parents now feel as though their student is now irretrievable – that she is too far gone already that she has lost herself somehow.

The Final Move

She just graduated from high school. She is too young to be written off this early in her life.

I'm writing this book for people like the last two students I just mentioned. I know they will want to take the nearest exit out of prison. I believe that they will identify with my story and be helped.

To appear to be successful to the world but to struggle on the inside is truly one of the worst prisons ever.

So what does "out" look like?

I will restate what I wrote in my introduction.

I'm quite comfortable with the skin I'm in. I'm more that OK with being a member of the black race. I like who I am and what I have become. The dread, fear and feeling of being trapped is now gone. As a matter of fact, very few people's negative _or_ positive opinions of me actually matter...

...And that feels very good. It's truly liberating. It is true freedom because there is no animosity associated with my liberty. Where there is no animosity and anger, there can be no strings that anyone can access to manipulate me the way a marionette controls a puppet.

I now have a different view of the world. While the world has changed, it has not changed enough in the areas that matter most. Oftentimes, a generation has to die off in order for the world's collective consciousness to change. For instance, we see more liberality in the way Americans choose a mate based on a changing of the guard. Overall, we have apathetic attitudes and the new unwritten rules in our society is, "mind your own business." There are just a small minority people who have truly had a heart change.

As I stated, the intent of this book is not to try and rid the world of racism; it's simply to tell my story with the hope that it would give someone hope and a chance to escape the hell I went through.

I didn't get better by becoming hateful.

I didn't get better by becoming a militant or by fighting back.

I didn't get better by sticking my head in the sand or by denying or attempting to deny my heritage.

I got better when I learned how to turn rules and religion into a relationship with God. I got better by understanding and educating myself on the human condition. I gained strength by looking inwardly and getting a proper perspective on my struggles – I realized that the purpose for my problems would prepare me for greatness and make me stronger. They were not designed to ruin my life and to destroy me. This changed me from being a victim to becoming a victor.

The Final Move

You may have noticed that I start each chapter with a microcosm of the nuggets I picked up along my journey through life. These are like gold to me I would not have made it to this point my life without them.

I was able to change through a constant diet of introspective reflection. Sad to say, I also had to learn from some really bad mistakes and from the wake of destruction I left in the form of damaged relationships and people where I was the either the perpetrator or the victim; in some cases I was both.

I had great friends and family that supported and carried me when I couldn't walk on my own. I had God's protection in response to the prayers of those same people.

Had it not been for all these things, I don't know where I'd be, but I doubt it would be in a good place.

Being exposed to a godly, spiritual atmosphere gave me a chance to parlay that information and those experiences into a real relationship with God. As I stated earlier, I could fill another book that is five times larger than the size of this book with stories that would illustrate my point.

But instead of filling up five more books how about one last story?

Most people have seen the movie, "Forrest Gump." It begins and ends with the same scene. Forrest is sitting on a park bench and the wind scoops up a feather from off the ground. The camera artistically captures it as it floats off. One day, I too found myself sitting on a bench in the park, around the corner from my beautiful home in the suburbs of Kansas. That day, no one could convince me that my life meant anything or that it would ever end up with me being happy. I felt unloved, unappreciated, and stuck. That day, my world came crashing in around me and I needed a miracle to be able to get up off that bench and to "soldier on."

I told God that no one loved me and that He knew how much that meant to me. Most people who know me know that I don't like clutter and trash. I saw some trash around me so I started picking it up. One piece of trash was a folded piece of paper with handwriting on it. My curiosity got the best of me and I opened it. Inside was the miracle I needed. The note said, "I love you."

Balderdash? Blind luck? Coincidence?

It would be too easy for you or me to explain it away and to dismiss it. But at that time, for me it was an answer. It was a rebuttal to my grief. It was divine intervention.

It was love. I know that the "true love conquers all" phrase has become cliché, but they are not my words, they are words that were written long ago by a man named Paul who has his own very interesting story. We believe his words were God-inspired and as a result, they have been canonized and placed in a collection of writings we now call the Holy Bible. The words are quotable and bear repeating.

And now abides faith, hope, love, these three; but the greatest of these is love. *(1 Corinthians 13:13, King James 2000 Bible)*

Love does conquer all, if you know where to look for it.

I would say your best opening move is to step away from your problems for moment, set this book down... rise slowly... and go help someone else. This action will take the magnifying glass off of you and your problems and at least give you an opportunity to catch your breath.

And remember, you have the final move.

The Conclusion of the Matter

I've lived a great life up to this point. It has been my distinct pleasure to have been given the opportunity to get up every day and be me. Is this the worst expository on the human condition that you've ever read? Hardly. Are there others who have suffered more? Certainly. But this is my story and I have written this small glimpse into my past and present in hopes that someone might be able to identify with my struggles. I write with the hope that my freedom from the effects of racism can be their freedom as well. More importantly, I pray that many will find the escape pod that will lead them away from a life of turmoil, low self-esteem and loss of identity and purpose.

No one wants to be a puppet or a pawn in life. That is, unless you are that special pawn in the endgame of life who is about to reach that all important 8th rank[10]. The self-awareness gained from a relationship with God, growing-up, and learning my purpose were the main things that positioned me for promotion and helped me to escape my own self-imposed prison. Time does not necessarily heal all wounds. Sometimes you have to implement a strategy for succeeding.

---

[10] A pawn that reaches the 8th rank during the course of a chess match can be promoted to a more powerful piece, usually a Queen.

References

Boyer, H. C. (1995). *The Golden Age of Gospel.* University of Illinois Press.

Frankl, V. E. (1946). *Man's Search for Meaning.* Vienna, Austria: Beacon Press .

John , E., & Taupin, B. (1975). Don't Let the Sun Go Down on Me [Recorded by E. John].

Landau, L. (Director). (1993). *Star Trek TNG, "Tapestry"* [Motion Picture].

Leventhal, E. M. (2012). *A Light from the Shadows: Reflections on Oneness, Identity, and the Creation of Experience.* Kihei, HI.

Polyp. (n.d.). *Under the Thumb, www.polyp.org.uk.*

Statement about Race at BJU. (2015). Retrieved from Bob Jones University: http://www.bju.edu/about/what-we-believe/race-statement.php

White, C. S. (1974). That's the Way of the World [Recorded by W. a. Earth].

Willis, H. (1946). The Psaltree Sermon. Roanoak, VA.

About the Author

Ray is an experienced lecturer and has an extensive track record of success in both the corporate and entrepreneurial marketplaces. Ray is a U.S. Air Force veteran and attended college at the University of Central Oklahoma in Edmond, OK. Ray is an avid sports enthusiast, likes to travel, is an accomplished musician, a voracious reader, and enjoys an occasional game of chess and/or a Star Trek Episode. Ray enjoys spending time with his family; wife Lorna Michelle, and four children – Shalanda, Cherrelle, Kenita and R.J.

About the Cover

The cover is a montage of my silhouette as a kindergartener (1964) and a famous endgame position in chess.

White is at a material disadvantage and should attempt to achieve a draw or a stalemate to win a half point. To do this, White needs to stay in front of Black's queening pawn before both of black's pieces reach this position. WK is on h8; BK is on h6 and Black's pawn is on g6.

Unfortunately, White ends up on the wrong side of Black's pawn. In this position with White to move:

- W: Kh8 – Kg8

- B: g6 – g7

- W: Kg8 – f7 (white's only legal move left)

- B: Kh6 – h7!

- W: Kf7 – whatever

- B: g7 – g8Q+

...and the chase is on. ***Black avoids a stalemate*** and can use the queen to drive White into a corner and deliver the checkmate. Normally, White would resign before getting to this final position.

Black

	a	b	c	d	e	f	g	h	
8	a8	b8	c8	d8	e8	f8	g8	h8	
7	a7	b7	c7	d7	e7	f7	g7	h7	
6	a6	b6	c6	d6	e6	f6	g6	h6	
5	a5	b5	c5	d5	e5	f5	g5	h5	
4	a4	b4	c4	d4	e4	f4	g4	h4	
3	a3	b3	c3	d3	e3	f3	g3	h3	
2	a2	b2	c2	d2	e2	f2	g2	h2	
1	a1	b1	c1	d1	e1	f1	g1	h1	
	a	b	c	d	e	f	g	h	

White

In a chess match with grandmasters, white would have an advantage since it gets the first move. White's objective is to achieve a win by checkmate and Black is trying to play defense in order to obtain a draw or a stalemate.

Made in the USA
Lexington, KY
17 September 2019